The MIDWIFE

The Birthing of a Seed of Greatness

Antenia M. Simmons

Bravin Publishing LLC, DE/NYC, USA

The Midwife
The Birthing of a Seed of Greatness

by

Antenia M. Simmons

Copyright © 2021

ISBN: 978-17355290-1-1

Library of Congress Number: 2021911299

Published by Bravin Publishing LLC

First Edition

All Scripture marked KJV is taken from the King James Bible version of the Bible.

Scripture marked NIV are taken from THE HOLY BIBLE, NEW INTERNATIONAL VERSION®, NIV® Copyright © 1973, 1978, 1984, 2011 by Biblica, Inc.® Used by permission. All rights reserved worldwide.

Scripture quotations marked AMP are taken from the Amplified® Bible (AMP), Copyright © 2015 by The Lockman Foundation. Used by permission. www.lockman.org

All Scripture quotations marked MSG are taken from THE MESSAGE, copyright © 1993, 2002, 2018 by Eugene H. Peterson. Used by permission of NavPress. All rights reserved. Represented by Tyndale House Publishers, Inc.

Scripture quotations marked NKJV are taken from the New King James Version®. Copyright © 1982 by Thomas Nelson. Used by permission. All rights reserved.

*This book is dedicated to my late Bishop,
David B. Gates II. For his leadership,
lessons on faith, and believing in me—
Bishop, you're forever in my heart.*

Table of Contents

1

Introduction

One of the best encounters people can have is recognizing both the gifts and purpose that God has formed in them. It's important to me to inspire others, to take the journey that will both water and flourish their seed of greatness.

God told Jeremiah that before He formed him in the womb, God knew him and He set him apart, appointing Jeremiah as a prophet to the nations. (Jeremiah 1:5, NIV) Based on God's revelation to Jeremiah, we can assume that God has not only given Jeremiah a gift and purpose, but He's also given everyone a purpose in the kingdom of God. Perhaps, not to be a prophet, but rather the call to be an apostle, evangelist, pastor, teacher, or some other gift to the world. (Ephesians 4:11, KJV)

Taking the steps to seek God to reveal your abilities will move God to assure you of your gifts. And then connecting to the role of a midwife will push you in the journey to fulfilling your purpose.

Naturally, a midwife has the responsibility of helping a woman during the labor and delivery process. Spiritually, when we take on the same responsibility as a midwife, then we can push the gifts and abilities that God has formed in us to come forth and fulfill its reason according to God's plan.

In Matthew 25:14-30, we hear a parable that symbolizes the value of gifts and purpose This parable begins with a master who distributed talents. To one, the master gave five talents; to the second he gave two, and to the third he gave one. Each were given talents according to their ability.

After the master gave them their talents, he asked them how they used them. Two out of the three said they used their talents for a purpose to please their master and to grow their gift. To them, the master said, *Well done.* However, when the third said he buried his talent, the master was not only displeased, but he took his talent away and gave it to another.

God, who is the master, wants you to use what He has formed in you and not to hide it.

Now, take a moment to think about the gifts God gave you. How can you use those gifts to both be a midwife and bring glory to God?

I believe most people have a huge desire to use what God has given them according to His plan, but because of the hard work and the perseverance it takes, we can become discouraged, settle, and give up.

But tell yourself, *Giving up is not an option.*

After you submit to God's will and God's word, you must keep pushing and encouraging yourself every day to have success with the seed of greatness God has given you, even when no one else encourages you.

Some days it will not be easy. You may not have someone consistently telling you that you can do it, that you have greatness in you, but it's during these times that you have to tell yourself to press forward and stay focused on the importance of giving birth to your seed, caring for your seed, and fulfilling your purpose.

> ***Philippians 3:13b-14*, NIV** – *Forget what is behind and strain toward what is ahead, and press on toward the goal to win the prize for which God has called you.*

Just like a mother in the delivery room, when it's minutes away from her baby entering into the world, the main word she hears is *push.*

Push, push. You can do it. Just keep pushing.

In the process of all that pushing, a mother is exhausted by an indescribable pain. However, as she pushes and presses, in due time, she gives birth to a beautiful baby. Just like in the delivery room, most levels of greatness don't come without great effort. Rewards and fulfillment don't come without a push.

This book is about challenging yourself to press and to push for your seed of greatness to come forth. You might have tried before and it didn't work the first time. You might have started a business and it failed. You might have went for that audition and were rejected. When you started your call to ministry, no one supported you.

But like Paul said, "Forget those things which are behind." (Philippians 3:13, KJV) Let go of the failures and disappointments that happened in the past and start again today.

Don't let your talent and purpose lie dormant because it didn't work the first time. It's easy to ponder on what went wrong and to blame others for our failures, but truthfully, no one can stop you from being successful and from being all God created you to be but you.

With faith, action, and determination, no one can kill your seed of greatness or stop it from growing.

Romans 8:31b says, "If God is for us, who can be against us." (NIV) Regardless of any setback, obstacle, or mountain, God is on your side. And with God on your side, you've got the biggest cheerleading squad that you can ever experience in a lifetime, with a power that no man can come against.

Say this to yourself: "I am a midwife. And no matter what, I will not let my seed of greatness and purpose die, but live."

Midwives have a responsibility to keep all babies on their watch alive and well. So, midwife, whether you're a male or female, keep pressing. David said in Psalm 118:17, "I will not die, but live to declare the works of the Lord." (KJV)

2

What Is Your Plan?

1 Corinthians 2:9, NKJV – *Eye has not seen, nor ear heard, / Nor have entered into the heart of man / The things which God has prepared for those who love Him.*

You may have already discovered both your purpose and the gifts that God has given you. You may even have a plan for your abilities.

I believe everyone should have a plan for their life. When you were younger, you may have been asked, "What, do you want to be when you grow up?" And now that you're older, "Where do you see yourself five years from now?"

These questions challenge us to have goals to accomplish great things for a positive purpose. I don't think anyone with the right mindset says they want to be unsuccessful, live in lack, have no kind of influence, or be a vessel that doesn't make a difference in the world.

I believe every human being wants to have a life of fulfillment with great achievements along the way. And perhaps you have made some accomplishments with the abilities that God gave you. But I ask you to think about this: Was the plan you made for your life the plan that God has made for you to live?

— 5 —

Ephesians 2:10, KJV – *We are God's workmanship, created in Christ Jesus unto good works which God hath ordained that we shall walk in them.*

The seeds of greatness that God gave you—meaning your gifts, your talents, your abilities, your strengths, and your uniqueness—was given to you by God with His plan for you to use them according to His will and way.

When I first discovered that I have been given the gift to be a playwright, and the ability to be an actress, I next began planning on how I wanted to use my gifts and talents—and it wasn't for ministry purposes. I dreamed and made goals of writing and traveling with my plays across the world full time. I dreamed of working with celebrities in sitcoms, while showcasing for theatre performances. And in my planning, I never thought to ask God what His plan was, or about how I should use the gifts He gave me.

I never thought there was anything wrong with the plans I made. After all, such goals were positive, with the intention of making honest money and doing what I love to do.

But because God created us for His work, I should have asked God for direction on what to do with what God formed in me.

Jeremiah 29:11, NIV – *"For I know the plans I have for you," declares the Lord, "plans to prosper you and not to harm you, plans to give you hope and a future."*

One day God revealed to me that what makes the seed of talents and abilities great is not the gift itself, but the outcome of our talents when we submit them to God. No matter what gift or ability God has given you, His overall plan and purpose is that you use what He has formed in you to bring

Him glory—to influence others to trust Him and to serve God as their Lord and Savior.

When God gave gifts to some to be apostles, prophets, evangelists, pastors, and teachers, He gave these gifts for the purpose of perfecting the saints, for the work of ministry, and for the edifying of the body of Christ. (Ephesians 4:11-12)

Perhaps you may not have been given any of the gifts mentioned in Ephesians 4:11-12. Nevertheless, whatever gift and talent God gave you, it has been given to you to use for the same reasons.

Who says that you can't use your gift for God's glory because you are a dancer, musician, artist, or one that operates with the gift of technology or creativity? Whoever says you can't is wrong!

David, a familiar name in the Bible, a man after God's own heart, was given a gift by God to skillfully play a harp. And due to David's gift, a king name Saul requested for David to consistently play for him. Whenever David used his gift to play, the evil spirits that tormented King Saul went away. (1 Samuel 16:14-23)

Notice, through David's skill as a musician, God doesn't only give seeds of greatness to prophets, pastors, and bishops. The gift God has given you has also been designed with unique greatness, purpose, and power through Christ.

Ephesians 3:20, KJV – *God is able to do exceedingly and abundantly above all that which we can ask or think according to the power that works in us.*

Relative to Ephesians 3:20, to experience God's power through your seed of greatness, you first have to be willing to submit to God's will and plan. When we submit to God's plan instead of ours, we will permanently experience a life of abundance. (John 10:10b). This doesn't mean that we will not experience trials along the way, but what's guaranteed is the final outcome of God's plan will be worth the process along with everlasting fulfillment.

You may think the plans you started for yourself are great and amazing, you may even be certain that your plan is satisfying. Such plans, like to be a doctor, get married and have a family, own a house, open a business, a studio or law firm, or even a plan to be a pilot. But after fulfilling your plan, how long will the satisfaction last? Will it be a permanent or a temporary fulfillment?

Mark 8:36 says, "What shall it profit a man to gain the whole world and loose his own soul?" (KJV) The plan of wholeness through God supersedes houses and cars. Millions of dollars in money, blue-collar and white-collar employment, and exposure to the world—to God, these accomplishments are small. And when we only reach to complete our plans of accomplishment, we sell ourselves short. However, when we submit to God the true manifestation of fulfillment and greatness operates and shines through our life.

In Luke 15:11-32, there is a parable of the Prodigal Son. I believe this story proves how submission to God's plan profits us more than the plans that we make.

The parable tells about a father that has two sons. One day, the younger son asks his father for his inheritance, and the father grants his son's request. Later on, the son goes away from home, gets lost in his way of life and squanders his inheritance. Eventually, when the son returns home, instead of the father being angry for his son's decision to leave and go his own way, the father (who represents Jesus Christ), forgives and celebrates his son for returning to the path that God predestined for him.

When the Prodigal Son went away from home to accomplish his plan, notice he was only temporary satisfied. However, when he returned back in the direction where God wanted him to be, he became permanently fulfilled.

It may seem better to handle life the way we want, but in the long run, we come out being made whole and truly happy when we submit to God's plan.

In Genesis 22, the Bible speaks of a man named Abraham. We read how he was tested by God to see if he would submit. God asked Abraham to sacrifice his son by having him killed as a burnt offering. This was Abraham's only son, whom I imagine he loved dearly, and wanted to live—like any parent would.

However, submission to God was Abraham's desire, even if it meant sacrificing his own son. Because ultimately, Abraham trusted God. The Bible also says that God ended up telling Abraham that he didn't have to submit his son as an offering, it was only a test to see his response. And because Abraham was willing, God promised him many blessings.

God told Abraham, "I will bless you, and in multiplying I will multiply your seed as the stars of the heaven, and as the sand which is on the seashore; and your seed shall possess the gate of his enemies; And in your seed shall all the nations of the earth be blessed; because you have obeyed My voice." (Genesis 22:17-18, KJV)

God's plan is the better choice. How has choosing your plan over God's caused you pain or regret in the past?

Along with the story of Abraham (Genesis 22) and the parable of the Prodigal Son. (Luke 15:11-32) God has proven through my life that submitting to His plan is a better choice.

As a writer, when I submitted my gift back to God, I didn't immediately see the type of results I wanted to see. As I began to write plays for ministry, the outcomes of the performances were excellent, but the budget, audience-numbers, and the vendors weren't exactly what I desired them to be. Yet, in time, God opened doors that began to connect with my dreams while I continue to write for God's glory.

I grew from having stage plays performed in youth centers and church basements with an audience of fifty, to presenting a stage play in a theatre with an audience capacity of one hundred forty-five—and the production was like no other.

God blessed me in many ways throughout this show. In fact, every single ticket sold out. 145 tickets were sold (Which was more than double of the amount of people I was used to seeing at any of my shows!) And to top all of that, people were giving monetary donations that I didn't even ask for— just to support the play.

God was definitely showing me what trusting Him can do. God blessed with me with an overflow of financial blessings for the production of the show's budget, and more importantly, the audience was blessed by the faith message in the performance.

Certainly, this was only the beginning of what God was showing me He can do with submission to Him. And I believe there's so much more that God has in store as I continue to trust and walk in His plan.

Do you choose God's plan or your plan? How has trusting your own plan hurt you in the past? How has trusting God's plan proven to you His faithfulness?

Submission to God's plan is not an easy choice. As human beings, our flesh will always war in battle between what it wants and the will of God. Galatians 5:17 says, "The flesh lusteth against the Spirit, and the Spirit against the flesh: and these are contrary the one to the other: so that ye cannot do the things that ye would." (KJV)

However, the decision to follow God's plan or your plan is a decision that has to be made. And God gives us a free will to choose. (Proverbs 16:9)

With a made-up mind of submission to God's plan, God's strength will help keep you focused on the path He has predestined for you. And in due season, success, prosperity, and the full manifestation of your seed of greatness will come forth.

For God told Joshua, "Be strong and courageous. Be careful to obey all the law ... Do not turn from it, to the right or to the left, that you may be careful to do everything written in it, then you will be prosperous and successful." (Joshua 1:7-8, NIV)

To be prosperous in the will of God, we must have both knowledge and understanding of how to work God's plan.

Proverbs 20:18, AMP – *Plans are established by counsel.*

Once you have said yes to God or have declared *not* your will, but God's will be done. The next step is to seek God's direction. Where there is no counsel on one's purpose, frustration will come.

How do your actions show (or not show) that having wisdom on God's will is a necessity?

In 1 Kings chapters 2-3, King Solomon requests prove that we need God's counsel to carry out His plan.

King Solomon had just been appointed by God to lead Israel. And one day, God appeared to Solomon in a dream, asking Solomon his desire. Solomon asked for wisdom on how to lead Israel. Notice, by Solomon asking for wisdom, this shows none of us can carry out the will of God without God's counsel. Whether you are called to pastor, to be a missionary, a worship leader or use some other gift, you need the wisdom of God. We cannot accomplish God's plan on our own ideology.

James said if any man lacks wisdom, let him ask of God, that gives to all men liberally and withholds judgement. (James 1:5)

Once you have asked God for direction and counsel on your seed of greatness, God will give you knowledge and understanding, leading you for God's will. (Proverbs 3:5-6)

God may not give you all that you need to know in one prayer session. We know that seeking God continuously for His plan is imperative. And when God doesn't answer your prayer right away, don't stop seeking Him. God's timing is not our timing. (2 Peter 3:8) With the Lord, a day is like a thousand years and a thousand years are like a day. At the appointed time, God will answer and give you clear instructions. (Habakkuk 2:3)

When Daniel prayed to God in Daniel 9, God's response to Him wasn't the same day that Daniel prayed. Instead, an angel of the Lord came to Daniel and said, "Do not be afraid, since the first day that you set your mind to gain an understanding and to humble yourself before God, your words were heard, and I have come in response to them." (Daniel 10:12, NIV)

Before the angel appeared, Daniel had to wait on God to speak. And during his time of waiting, he was mourning and eating nothing for three full weeks. (Daniel 10:2-3) But in God's timing, God responded.

Just like Daniel, sometimes God will have us waiting. And we may have to wait on God during difficult and life-changing times—but it's during these times God is teaching us to trust Him the most.

No matter how long it takes for God to answer, wait on Him. What are 2-3 things you can do while you wait on that response to show that you're trusting God?

Waiting on God to answer may not be popular. I myself do not like waiting too long in any situation. Yet, the fruit of patience (Galatians 5:23-25) is truly needed for this journey with God. I believe patience prevents making hasty decisions that do not work out for our good and or in our favor. However, wrong decisions can be prevented if we become disciplined in waiting on God's direction to show us His plan, that we may be in God's perfect will and not in His permissible will—the will God permits based on your choice. (Dictionary)

"God's permissible will does not have the full blessings."

Choose God's plan. Seek God's counsel. Wait on God to answer.

3

The Process

Philippians 1:6, KJV – And I am sure of this, that he who began a good work in you will bring it to completion at the day of Jesus Christ.

Once you have sought God's plan for your life, you will need to go through a process—a series of actions or steps taken in order to achieve a particular end. (Dictionary)

I personally don't always like the process required for achieving most goals. However, I understand that anything of value doesn't develop overnight, and a process of necessary steps is required before achieving levels of greatness.

For instance, studies shows that a diamond is worth anywhere between $2,500 to $18,000 per carat. And a diamond only develops with a process of high pressure and temperature, with a time frame of 1 billion to 3.3 billion years to complete. (Geology.com)

Similar to the development of a diamond, individually we may have to experience tests that are equivalent to the feeling of high pressure and high temperatures. And in the process of tests and pressure, discouragement may come especially when it feels like the process of pressure is too long. But during these times, speak over yourself and say, "I won't get distracted by the pressure, I shall come forth."

I Corinthians 10:13 declares that God will never give us more than we can bear. Therefore, by this promise, we can trust that the process that God has set for each of us is not meant to destroy us, but to position us to produce what we are created to do with the power of God.

For the process of suffering develops the anointing. When have you endured the process of suffering? What anointing do you think was being developed during this time?

When Jesus was in the process of fulfilling his purpose of dying on the cross for the remission of our sins (Romans 5:8), not all moments of His process were comfortable. Before the day of Jesus' sacrifice, Luke 9:22 says the son of man must suffer many things and be rejected by the elders and chief priests and scribes and be killed to die..."

Surely the suffering of Jesus' purpose to save us was a process of pain, but if Christ did not stay in place during the process, the will of God would not have been fulfilled, nor the power of God through Jesus be with us today. 1 Corinthians 15:3-4 says after Christ died, it was three days later that He was raised from the dead with all power in His hands. And Jesus Christ was declared to be the son of God with power after He completed His process of suffering.

__1 Peter 5:10, KJV__ – For the God of all grace, who called us to his eternal Glory in Christ, after ye have suffered a little while, make you perfect, establish, strengthen, and settle you.

— 16 —

Based on 1 Peter 5:10, I believe the pain that comes within a process is not easy. However, I also believe to endure any suffering for Christ's sake is worth it, due to the power that God gives in exchange.

I learned in church, "The anointing makes the difference." And although this is a cliché, I find these words to be true. My parents raised me in church, but I wasn't saved all my life. I have experienced serving in church with and without the anointing of God. And it wasn't until I accepted Christ as my savior and entered into a process in Christ that I learned just how effective the anointing of God really is.

The anointing of God is defined as, "The burden removing and yoke breaking power of God, which empowers a man or woman to function supernaturally."[1] The anointing of God enables every work and every perfect gift from God to function effectively.

While your gift(s) may look good on you, and even sound good to others, the anointing of God is necessary for a reason. Without the power of God, your gift(s) and callings cannot carry out God's perfect will to edify, perform miracles, deliver, heal, and draw others unto salvation.

> ***Luke 4:18*** *– The spirit of the Lord is upon me because he has anointed me to proclaim good news to the poor. He has sent me to proclaim liberty to the captives and recovering of sight to the blind and to set at Liberty those who are oppressed.*

Relative to Luke 4:18, everyone that chooses to be submissive to God's plan needs to have the power of God upon their

---

[1] https://www.murrayledger.com

— 17 —

life. Whether one's purpose be to serve from the pulpit, the church, kitchen, or in the music, usher, or children's ministry, the power of God is imperative to perform great works and to proclaim the works of God.

Everyone may have been given a purpose, gift, or ability by God, but not everyone's ability has been anointed by God. Have you asked God for His anointing power on your gifts?

Gifts and callings of God come without repentance (Romans 11:29). However, obtaining the power of God does not come without paying the price tag of either suffering for righteousness' sake (1 Peter 3:14), and/or by enduring a process of preparation and testing to accomplish God's plan.

The anointing of God can come either before or after the process. Where are you in the process right now?

Although Jesus Christ received all power in His hands, after He endured His process of crucifixion, unlike Jesus, sometimes God may anoint us with His power, not after the process but before.

In 1 Samuel 16–17, it demonstrates how God can anoint us first and then take us through a process of preparation and testing before He uses us for a particular purpose. In this text (1 Samuel 16-17), there's a man named David and another man name Saul. Unlike Saul, David was a man after God's own heart, not tall in stature, and not considered to have the look of a king.

However, God still chose David and had him anointed at the age of seventeen to be the next king, not based on his outward appearance, but based on David's heart (1 Samuel 16:7).

Saul, who was already king of Israel, was set to be replaced by David because of Saul's disobedience. Saul disobeyed God by not following God's command to destroy the Amalekites (1 Samuel 15:1-9). Saul also disobeyed God by not waiting in Gilgal for seven days for Samuel to return for the sacrificing of burnt and peace offerings, like he had been instructed to do. (KJV)

By Saul's disobedience, it teaches God is merciful, yet constant disobedience will eventually cause us to lose the power and anointing of God that we need to reach our full potential in Him.

When Samuel disobeyed God the first time, God gave him another chance. But after the second time, Saul lost his anointing and was destined to be replaced by David as king. For Saul to lose his kingship was a big consequence, but losing his anointing was much more of a severe punishment.

Once the spirit of the lord was no longer with Saul, although he was still King of Israel, he no longer had power to defeat his enemies. The Bible says in 1 Samuel 16:14, "When the spirit of the Lord departed from Saul an evil spirt from the Lord troubled him." (KJV)

Relative to 1 Samuel 15:1-9 and I Samuel 16:14, I personally can deal with being sat down from a position in a ministry because of my disobedience, but what would really hurt me more is if the Lord took away my anointing. Because the power of God not only makes our gift(s) and calling effective while assuring the spirit of the Lord is with us, but the anointing also destroys the enemy and gives us protection in the process. This is why I believe in David's case, God anointed him before his process so that he would be protected from any attack.

Like David, before the appointed time you are to operate in your gift and or calling, perhaps God will anoint you ahead of time to protect you from what lies ahead in your process to fulfilling your purpose.

When Samuel took the horn of the oil and anointed him to be king, David was 17 years old, but didn't sit on the throne as king until age thirty. And I imagine David had no idea what lay ahead of him. But God knew, therefore when David was anointed (1 Samuel 17: 34-35), the spirit of the Lord came mightily upon him from that day forward (1 Samuel 16: 13-14, AMP). And with the power of God, it protected David and gave David strength for battle (1 Samuel 17: 31). The same day David had been anointed, he started his process of preparation.

The process of preparation is what God takes everyone through. Where are you at right now in your process of preparation?

For the steps that God has us to go through in a process of preparation, are meant to make us ready for our God-given assignments, that we would be able to handle the different encounters that will come while fulfilling our purpose.

The Lord doesn't just bless us in our gift(s) and our purpose in life for our own pleasure, but there is a reason behind why God chose you to fulfill a work for Him. And the more gifts and abilities and anointing you have been given by God, the more which will be required from you. Luke 12:48 says to whom much is given, much is required. Therefore, whatever God requires from you, you're going to have to be prepared to fulfill.

I believe this is why after David was anointed to be the next king, it wasn't until thirteen years later he sat on the throne.

Because God had to make sure David was ready for the toss and turns that came with being a king of Israel. David needed to be trained to trust God and to rely on God for leading and direction. To be a king was a huge assignment. And David had the chance to be properly trained to be king, through situations of warfare and testing.

When David was underestimated by his father Jessie as the one chosen by God, this was the day, that David's process of preparation began. (1 Samuel 16) The same day David was underestimated by Jessie was the same day David was anointed by Samuel to be the next king.

By David being underestimated, this beginning process enabled David to grow in faith by relying on God and not depending on validation from people. David had to learn in the beginning of his process that there would be people close to him that would not believe in him—even family.

One of the hardest parts in a process of God's will is recognizing that the people we want to believe in us and to genuinely support us will not always do so. However, it's in the preparation process that God showed David and God shows us that it's better to put our confidence in God than in man.

David said it himself in Psalm 118:8: "It is better to trust in the Lord than to put confidence in man." (KJV)

By David writing Psalm 118:8, David showed in his process of preparation that he understood, that trusting God more than anyone else was the way to endure any assignment by God.

*Confidence in God helps us endure and overcome the process.
Where are you putting your confidence?*

In 1 Samuel 17, David proves his trust in God as he goes into battle against a Philistine named Goliath (1 Samuel 17: 48-49). Goliath was described as a giant who was ten feet tall. He challenged King Saul to pick anyone from Israel's troops to fight against him.

When David arrived on the scene (to bring his brothers food and to check on them), God used the encounter involving Goliath to prepare him for times of battle, to use both faith and the power of God.

When David saw how frightened the Israelites were after Goliath's challenge to fight (1 Samuel 17:32), he volunteered to fight Goliath with confidence in God and faith he could destroy Goliath with his anointing.

I believe any time God has us in spiritual warfare against our adversaries, the key to overcoming every attack and fiery dart is with the power of God. David wrote in Psalm 24:8, "Who is the King of glory? The Lord strong and mighty, the Lord mighty in battle." (NIV)

David was confident that God would use him to defeat Goliath, even though both David's brother and Saul doubted that David could. Saul shared that David was too young and wasn't experienced. However, despite those who didn't believe in him, David already learned in the beginning of his process that man's approval is not necessary to do the work of God.

If God chose you to be the woman or man for the assignment, then it matters not who believes, as long as you

— 22 —

believe what God says about you. Similar to David, we can't let naysayers stop us from believing God and fulfilling the plan God has for us.

Since the spirit of the Lord was with David, that was all the power he needed to do what God had already predestined for him to do in the battle against Goliath. Tell yourself you can do what seems impossible with faith and the power of God.

Along with faith and God's power, when David fought Goliath, David selected five stones and said to the Philistine (1 Samuel 17:45), "You come at me with a sword. but I come at you in the name of the Lord of hosts."

> ***Zechariah 4:6, KJV*** *– Not by might nor by power, but by my Spirit,' says the Lord Almighty.*

When David defeated Goliath, not only did he prove his doubters wrong, but this victory made a clear statement—that God was with David and the anointing of God is more powerful than any other power. David said in Psalm 20:7, "For some trust in chariots, and some trust in horses, but we will remember the name of the Lord our God." (AMP)

The victory David had won in his battle with Goliath prepared David even more to continue to trust God, recognizing that no matter what other battles came later on when he became king, he could be sure that if God could save him from an enemy such as Goliath, then God could save him again from anything or anyone else in his future.

Like David, at times in our process of preparation, we will encounter battles. Some battles we will view as being sweatless, and other battles will seem too hard to face. However, we can be sure that if God brought us out of one hard place, then surely God can do it again. Tell yourself, trust God, before, during, and even after the process.

When David won against Goliath, he also passed his process of preparation. However, David still had to go through another process called testing.

If you can pass the process of preparation, then you can pass the process of testing. Are you willing to pass the process of preparation by remembering all that God has done for you?

Naturally, any time we are given a test, a procedure intended to establish the quality of our knowledge, performance, or reliability (Google Dictionary), whether in school, from an employer, or by God, the test may not be easy.

However, when taking and enduring a test, it proves our ability and determination. Spiritually when we take and endure a test by God, it proves that our faith in Him is true, and that we are steadfast and unmovable with a mind to abound in the work of the Lord. 1 Peter 1:7-9 says, "These trials will show that your faith is genuine. It is being tested as fire tests and purifies gold—though your faith is far more precious than mere gold. So, when your faith remains strong through many trials, it will bring you much praise and glory and honor on the day when Jesus Christ is revealed to the whole world." (NLT)

Relative to I Peter 1:7, after David learned in his process of preparation to trust and depend on God, his faith had to be tested. And David's testing began when King Saul turned against him.

The Bible shows that Saul became jealous of David in 1 Samuel 18:6-16. When women poured out of all the villages of Israel singing and dancing, welcoming king Saul with tambourines, festive songs, and lutes, singing Saul kills by the thousand, and David by the ten thousand, this caused Saul to become angry and jealous.

The next day, an evil spirit was sent by God to afflict Saul, and Saul became quite beside himself, raving. David played his harp, as he usually did at such times. Only this time, Saul threw a spear, thinking he would "nail David to the wall." (1 Samuel 19:9, KJV)

Although God sent this evil spirit on Saul to test David (1 Samuel 19:9), Saul's plans to kill David didn't work. When the spear Saul used missed David, Saul saw clearly that the anointing was still on David's life, and that David was protected from his jealous evil spirit.

However, as Saul saw David becoming more successful, he himself became more jealous and he set up another trap for David. This time, Saul made David an officer in Israel's army so David would be killed (1 Samuel 18:13). But, once again, God protected David from Saul, and while protecting David, God was helping David to endure his test.

For although God uses principalities and wickedness in high places to test us, God gives us a way of escape (1 Corinthians 10:13).

When God sends a test, He may not give us an idea of when the test is coming or who the test is coming through, but God did promise that testing will come, and He will provide a way for us to endure.

1 Corinthians 10:13, KJV – There hath no temptation taken you but such as is common to man: but God is faithful, who will not suffer you to be tempted above that ye are able; but will with the temptation also make a way to escape, that ye may be able to bear it.

Any time I am tested through an encounter sent by God, God gives me a choice to take His way of escape by trusting Him and relying on Him to see me through, or I can choose to handle my encounter my own way and fail the test.

In 1 Samuel 18:10, the day God sent an evil spirit on Saul against David, this situation was not only a test of faith, but also a test of David's endurance.

"Be assured that the testing of your faith produces endurance." (James 1:3, AMP) Have you ever tried to handle a test of God your own way?

David could have handled this attack from Saul in His own way. However, by David not taking matters into his own hands, this proved in the beginning of his process of testing that his faith was still strong in God, and that he could endure suffering for the will of God.

I commend David for the suffering that he endured in his testing for both faith and endurance. I imagine that although David endured Saul's attacks, he also had to endure the hurt from knowing the same person he was helping was the same person that was trying to kill him.

Similar to David, in the process of testing, God may use people you work with, the closest people to you, and or people you have confided in, to come against you, and this is what causes the pain of suffering the most. However, David shows by example in response to Saul, don't let your faith waiver, but endure the test. And by David's example of strong faith, he passed the test of both faith and endurance with flying colors.

I'm certain, David was able to see that the test he was taking was not meant to destroy him but to make him stronger. 1 Peter 5:10 reminds us that even in our encounters of suffering within our process, God's power is making us strong, steadfast, and preparing us to fulfill our purpose.

1 Peter 5:10, KJV – But the God of all grace, who hath called us unto his eternal glory by Christ Jesus, after that ye have suffered a while, make you perfect, stablish, strengthen, settle you."

I give you 1 Peter 5:10 again, as when we are in the process of testing, we should stand on this Scripture to keep us mindful that although the process of testing may be painful, in the end, it will make us better and glad.

For we are to count it all joy when we meet trials of various kinds. (James 1:2) For God knows the way we are to take when He has tried us, we shall come forth as pure gold. (Job 23:10)

Based on Job 23:10, God's word confirms that we can't skip the process God has for us to take and expect to come forth with greatness and our purpose in Him. Tell yourself, *I need the process.*

Like David, we will have to go through a process of testing to test our faith, endurance, and lastly, a process to test our character.

The test of character is the final challenge in our process. How is your character being tested right now?

Matthew 16:24 says, "Then Jesus said to his disciples "Whoever wants to be my disciple must deny themselves and take up their cross and follow me." (NIV)

Relative to Matthew 16:24, denying the flesh means to not give in to our sinful nature and selfish pleasures. However, when we take up the cross of Jesus and follow God's ways, then we represent the integrity and righteousness that God requires in his plan for us.

When God tests our character, meaning our morals, the way we think and behave, God is checking if we will act according to his will or according to our flesh.

My mother raised me to think that the same way you eat at the dinner table at home will be the same way you will eat when you're out in a public. Therefore, I think this same concept applies relative to when we are in process of testing. How we behave in our test of character will show ourselves and God how we will act in our purpose, calling, and position in the body of Christ.

In 1 Samuel 18:14, when David was first attacked by Saul, the Scripture says, "David behaved himself wisely in all his ways; and the Lord was with him." (KJV) For by David behaving wisely in this encounter, I gather that when the appointed time came for David to sit on the throne as king, he would act wisely by denying the flesh and remaining humble unto God.

Denying the flesh in response to an encounter similar to David, such as an attack from an individual or spiritual warfare, is not always easy. Even the kindest, most honest, and patient person can be tempted to respond to the enemy in their flesh. In other words, with strife, retaliation, and evil.

— 28 —

However, I believe the two ways to pass a test of character is by one, understanding that as long as you respond the way Christ leads, your purpose will be protected and fulfilled, and two, by prayer and supplication. (Ephesians 6:18)

In Psalm 25:21, David prayed, "May integrity and uprightness protect me, because my hope, Lord is in you. In other words I gathered David is saying, when any circumstance would come up against him, If he continues to behave in a righteous and upright way, he can trust that God would protect him and his purpose to be King of Israel." (NIV)

Although David endured and overcame the first two traps by Saul, there was still another attack Saul sent against David. After David conquered Saul's setup when he assigned him to be a commander in Israel's army, David started back working for Saul in the palace as a harp player. And lo and behold, Saul tried to kill David while David was playing the harp—only this time David ran away and went into hiding. (1 Samuel 19: 9-10 KJV)

Based on these three attacks by Saul, any human being, including myself, would have by the third attack became worried, afraid, or ready to repay Saul back evil for evil. But David passed this test of character by prayer and supplication.

Ephesians 6:18 says, "Praying always with all prayer and supplication in the Spirit, and watching thereunto with all perseverance and supplication for all saints." (KJV) Are you willing to deny your flesh during tests of character?

David prayed in Psalm 27:

The LORD *is my light and my salvation; whom shall I fear? the* LORD *is the strength of my life; of whom shall I be afraid?*

When the wicked, even mine enemies and my foes, came upon me to eat up my flesh, they stumbled and fell.

Though an host should encamp against me, my heart shall not fear: though war should rise against me, in this will I be confident.

One thing have I desired of the LORD, *that will I seek after; that I may dwell in the house of the* LORD *all the days of my life, to behold the beauty of the* LORD, *and to enquire in his temple.*

For in the time of trouble he shall hide me in his pavilion: in the secret of his tabernacle shall he hide me; he shall set me up upon a rock.

And now shall mine head be lifted up above mine enemies round about me: therefore will I offer in his tabernacle sacrifices of joy; I will sing, yea, I will sing praises unto the LORD.

Hear, O LORD, *when I cry with my voice: have mercy also upon me, and answer me.*

When thou saidst, Seek ye my face; my heart said unto thee, Thy face, LORD, *will I seek.*

Hide not thy face far from me; put not thy servant away in anger: thou hast been my help; leave me not, neither forsake me, O God of my salvation.

*When my father and my mother forsake me, then the LORD
will take me up.*

*Teach me thy way, O LORD, and lead me in a plain path,
because of mine enemies.*

*Deliver me not over unto the will of mine enemies: for false
witnesses are risen up against me, and such as breathe out
cruelty.*

*I had fainted, unless I had believed to see the goodness of the
LORD in the land of the living.*

*Wait on the LORD: be of good courage, and he shall
strengthen thine heart: wait, I say, on the LORD." (KJV)*

Notice in this Psalm that as David prayed, he may have been
afraid because of Saul's efforts of trying to kill him, he clearly
understood that there was safety and strength at the altar of
God.

David still trusted in God even as God continue to challenge
him through this process. The more David cried out to God
in Psalm 27 the more David showed that he realized to make
it through his process he was going to need God to lead him
as he prayed.

Psalm 27:11, NIV – *Teach me thy way, O Lord, and
lead me in a plain path, because of mine enemies.*

Similar to how David cried out to God in prayer, we need to
do the same also. Prayer, I repeat, is the way to pass a test of
character. If we don't communicate with God in our process,
we won't have the strength to deny our flesh and follow
God's upright way.

For instance, think about a day you didn't start your day off with prayer. How did you respond to others and behave through the day? Were you easily short-tempered, unforgiving, or behaving with a nasty disposition?

When we examine how we act and pray accordingly, we should see a difference in our behavior and our response to the trials and tests by God.

By David praying in his final test of character, and with his last response to Saul's attack against him, he proved that prayer works if you're willing to deny the flesh and take up your cross and follow God's plan.

In Samuel 24, we can see through David that prayer works. When Saul found out where David was hiding, Saul set out to have David found. While looking for David, Saul saw a cave and he went inside to cover his feet. Meanwhile, David and the men with him were huddled far back in the same cave.

And when the men saw Saul, they said unto David, "Behold the day of which the Lord said unto thee, Behold, I will deliver thine enemy into thine hand, that thou mayst do to him as it shall seem good unto thee." (1 Samuel 24:4, KJV) For David had a choice to handle Saul his way or the way of the Lord. And this was David's chance to ultimately pass his test or fail.

In Samuel 24:6-7, it says David decided to arise and cut off the skirt of Saul's robe. I believe by cutting a portion of Saul's robe, this meant David possibly contemplated killing Saul. But David's strength in God restrained him from doing so.

I Samuel 24:6-7 tells us that after David had cut off Saul's skirt, he told His men the Lord forbid that he should do this thing to his master. David told his servants not to rise against Saul, and Saul rose out of the cave and went on his way.

1 Samuel 24:8 — David also arose afterward, and went out of the cave, and cried after Saul, saying, My lord the king. And when Saul looked behind him, David stooped with his face to the earth, and bowed himself. And David said to Saul, Wherefore hearest thou men's words, saying, Behold, David seeketh thy hurt? Behold, this day thine eyes have seen how that the Lord had delivered thee to day into mine hand in the cave: and some bade me kill thee: but mine eye spared thee; and I said, I will not put forth mine hand against my lord.; for he is the Lord's anointed.

1 Samuel 16-20 tells us:

And it came to pass, when David had made an end of speaking these words unto Saul, that Saul said, Is this thy voice, my son David? And Saul lifted up his voice, and wept. And he said to David, Thou art more righteous than I: for thou hast rewarded me good, whereas I have rewarded thee evil. And thou hast shewed this day how that thou hast dealt well with me: forasmuch as when the Lord had delivered me into thine hand, thou killest me not. For if a man find his enemy, will he let him go well away? wherefore the Lord reward thee good for that thou hast done unto me this day. And now, behold, I know well that thou shalt surely be king, and that the kingdom of Israel shall be established in thine hand. (KJV)

Relative to 1 Samuel 16, when Saul honored David because of David's choice not to kill him in spite of his attacks, Saul saw that David was prepared to be a good king, and that he had been defeated by a person with good character. Perhaps

Saul also realized that David would be a stronger and wiser king than he.

By David being willing to deny his flesh, pray, and to listen to the instructions of God, shows us it was certainly the strength of God and the light of God that David used to defeat Saul.

For when we follow God and allow God to fight for us in our process of testing, we can do more harm to our enemies than when we try to fight the enemy in our own way.

Although it was God who sent the affliction upon David's life through Saul's evil spirit, it was God who delivered David out of the affliction Psalm 34:19 says, "Many are the afflictions of the righteous: but the LORD delivereth him out of them all." (KJV)

When David chose not to kill Saul, he passed his test of character and was delivered from his affliction. Based on the outcome of David's process of preparation, testing of faith, endurance and testing of character, you should be confident that in your process, like David, you can pass and make it through with the anointing of God.

When we deny our flesh, trust God, pray, and follow God's leading, regardless of any circumstance or attack, we can come forth with our abilities, fulfill our purpose, and have a strong finish.

__Deuteronomy 31:8 (NIV)__ – The Lord himself goes before you and will be with you; he will never leave you nor forsake you. Do not be afraid; do not be discouraged.

Stand on God's word and be confident because God is with you, even in the process.

Decree and declare, "I am a midwife and no matter what; I will not let my seed of greatness die, but live."

4

Push

Philippians 3:14, KJV – *Press toward the mark for the prize of the high Calling of God in Christ Jesus.*

Ecclesiastes 3:1 says, "To every thing there is a season, and a time to every purpose under the heaven:" (KJV) Therefore, in each season in your journey to fulfilling your purpose you will encounter changes along the way. And because of these changes, there will be times where you will need to push. Merriam-Webster dictionary says the word "push" means to press or urge forward to completion.

As I discussed in the previous chapter, going through a process is a part of the journey to fulfilling your purpose, and in addition to this, also a time where we will have to press in encouraging our self, press in prayer, and press in using God's Word to fulfill our purpose.

In our journey in fulfilling our purpose, we should be also mindful that we will experience seasons that will involve going through times of discouragement, valley experiences, correction from God, and waiting on the promises of the Lord. And during these difficult seasons, I believe in order to stay strong in faith, steadfast, and unmovable in the work of

— 36 —

the Lord, we should first rely on the ability to encourage our self in the Lord.

Push by encouraging yourself. Where do you need to encourage yourself right now?

Naturally, everyone wants a cheerleader by their side either for encouragement or for support. Such as a mother that is pregnant with a child, of course she wouldn't want to go through the journey of giving birth alone. For in most cases, I believe the mother's desire throughout the pregnancy is to have the support of the father and loved ones with her, during the planning, on doctor visits, and especially with her in the delivery room.

And like in the natural, spiritually, when we are on our journey to fulfilling our purpose, we want people with us during each season to believe in us and to help push us.

However, I realized while being on my journey to fulfilling my purpose in God that the idea of your "support team" being able to push your movement in your course with God will be limited and unreliable. There will be times where God will have us not just isolated, but separated from our support team because it's not God's will that your friends and loved ones be able to go with you in every season of your journey. Therefore, it's imperative to become disciplined in encouraging yourself in the Lord.

In 1 Samuel 30, when David was king of Israel, the Amalekites (enemies of Israel) had made an attack on a town called Ziklag. The Amalekites destroyed this site with fire, kidnapped the women and the children that were present, and held them in captivity. Once David arrived on the scene and saw what had happened, he became distressed because the people appeared to blame him, and wanted him stoned for what the Amalekites had done.

However, in 1 Samuel 30:6b, it says that David encouraged himself in the Lord. When David arrived to Ziklag, he had his army with him, but he couldn't rely on a close friend, such as Johnathan, to encourage him because he had died in battle against the Philistines. (1 Samuel 31) It also says he couldn't rely on his wives Haynam and Abigail to encourage him because at Ziklag they had been captured and brought into captivity by the Amalekites.

During such a time of discouragement because his friend and wives had been limited by God on when they would be with David, David had to press past the distress he felt and push towards the Lord with is own words of encouragement. David said to himself in Psalm 43:5, "Why art thou cast down, O my soul? and why art thou disquieted within me? Hope in God: for I shall yet praise him, who is the health of my countenance, and my God." (KJV)

Based on Psalm 43:5, it's clear that David's spirit was cast down—possibly because of his circumstances in Ziklag however, by David encouraging himself, he was able to lift himself up to continue to put his hope in God and push in his purpose as king of Israel.

David has shown in Psalm 43:5 that when we are feeling cast down, one way to defeat a spirit of oppression and loss of hope is by speaking to our self the hope of God with an offering of praise unto the Lord. However, this is just one way to encourage yourself in the Lord. Another way I believe is by saying a fervent prayer.

Although prayer is simply defined as our direct line to heaven that allows us to communicate with God, fervent prayer is another level of prayer that can push our spirit to reach God for breakthrough, strength, and a manifestation of God's will. (Galatians 4:19)

For we can be confident when approaching God that if we ask anything according to His will, He hears us. (1 John 5:14) And the effectual fervent prayer of a righteous man avails much. (James 5:16b)

Therefore, based on these Scriptures (I John 5:14 and James 5:16b), we can be certain, travailing (pushing in prayer) to encourage our self is effective and not a waste of time. For men are to always pray and not faint (Luke 18:1), and to pray without ceasing (1 Thessalonians 5:17). Therefore, no matter what seasons of discouragement or pain we encounter, we should strive to not let go of the horns of the altar, but rather pray and press in prayer.

In Samuel 1: 1-18 is an example of a woman that prayed a fervent prayer during the time when her spirit was in oppression and anguish. This woman, Hannah, was in anguish because she was unable to have children, for the Lord had shut up her womb. Hannah was one of the wives married to Elkanah, and Peninnah was the name of Elkanah other wife who could have children. And Peninnah reminded Hannah every time she could, by provoking Hannah to make her fret because she was barren.

Elkanah however, loved Hannah and favored her more. It didn't matter to him that Hannah could not give birth. But being barren did discourage Hannah, and it made her bitter.

One day Hannah, went to the temple to pray, not taking anyone with her. She privately asked God to look upon her affliction and to give her a son. She vowed if God answered her prayer, she would give her son back to God for His will.

After Hannah made this vow unto God, she cried out to God with all the anguish that was in her heart. From her heart flowed a lot of pain—the hurt from being provoked by Peninnah, the hurt and possible shame felt due to being barren, and the sorrow from being discouraged.

Yet, when Hannah prayed, it's evident that she pushed fervently unto God. 1 Samuel 1:12-13 says, "And it came to pass, as she continued praying before the Lord, that Eli (a priest by the temple) marked her mouth. Now Hannah, she spake in her heart; only her lips moved, but her voice was not heard: therefore, Eli thought she had been drunken." (KJV)

Based on verse 13, where it's written Eli thought Hannah had been drunken, I thought of how someone behaves when drunk. Usually, there is no control of self, one is overcome by an emotion, and out of their usual behavior. Therefore, for Eli to think Hannah was drunk, it symbolizes that Hannah prayed until she lost control and the spirit of God then took control of her perspective, her heart, and her soul.

> *1 Samuel 1:14, KJV – And Hannah answered and said
> No, my lord (Eli), I am a woman of a sorrowful spirit: I
> have drunk neither wine nor a strong drink, but have poured
> out my soul before the Lord.*

Relative to verse 14, Hannah makes it clear that in her communication with God, she cast her cares on Him, and released her gloom and anguish so that God would have His way in her heart. Hannah not only desired a son, but she wanted to be delivered from her sorrowful spirit.

For anytime we are in a place of discouragement, recognize it can lead to a place of bondage, and when bound by a sorrowful and or a depressed state, deliverance is needed in order to get back up and move on in fulfilling one's purpose in God.

Galatians 5:1 says, "Stand fast therefore in the liberty wherewith Christ hath made us free, and be not entangled again with the yoke of bondage." (KJV) It is not God's will that we be bound by a spirit of heaviness. For Isaiah 61:3 says, "For the spirit of heaviness put on the garment of praise that we may be called trees of righteousness, that God might be glorified." (KJV)

In order to keep moving in our journey to fulfilling our purpose, we can't afford to waste time and settle in discouragement too long. Yes, there's a time to cry, but we have to know when it's time to press past the low place and allow God to set us free from who or what caused us to be cast down.

Tell yourself, "I won't miss my elevation to greatness over a pity party." For Hannah was delivered from her distress because she let go and pushed through until there was a breakthrough.

In Samuel 1:17 -18, after Hannah prayed, Eli told her to go in peace. He spoke for the God of Israel to grant her the petition that she had asked God for. Then Hannah went her way and her countenance was no sadder.

I love that 1 Samuel 1:17 mentions that Hannah's countenance was no longer sad. By Hannah's countenance being changed, this proves that Hannah prayed until everything that was weighing her down and causing her pain was no longer in her heart. For her soul had been lifted, and she walked away from the temple free and with a countenance that showed that she was also believing God for a son.

Hannah shows in 1 Samuel 1:12-18 that travailing in prayer can break the barriers that are meant to hinder us from coming forth with our purpose. Such as barriers of offense, bitterness, disappointment, or discouragement. And, if currently these are barriers that you are struggling with, it's nothing to be ashamed of. These are realistic barriers that everyone has faced, and if there is a person that hasn't, well I would say keep on living.

More importantly, is that after recognizing these barriers in your life, you must spiritually push your barriers to come down.

Donald Lawrence wrote a song lyric that says "Giants do fall." I'm telling you, that the barriers that stem from discouragement don't have to be your stumbling block. Such barriers can be defeated.

> **Matthew 7:7-8, KJV** – *Ask and it shall be given you, seek and ye shall find, knock and it shall be opened unto you.*

When our heart is heavy from the circumstances along the way of doing God's will, we can certainly pour out to God and ask God for help. For David said, "I will lift up mine eyes to the hills from whence cometh my help, my help comes from the Lord who made heaven and earth." (Psalm 121:1-2, KJV)

We may not always have our best friend or family to encourage us on our journey to fulfilling our purpose, but we have God. God not only hears us, but He is with us. Matthew 28:20b says, "And lo, I am with you always, even unto the end of the world." (KJV)

Thank God that He is always with us, and thank God that we don't need someone else to pray for us in order for God to bring us through. We can go directly to God for our self and travail in prayer and get powerful, life-changing results. Besides, there's no friend or family member that can understand our tears and our groaning like God can.

Such as in 1 Samuel 1:8, when Hannah wept over being barren, her husband asked her why she was weeping and why her heart was grieved. Then he said, "Am I not better to thee than ten sons?"

He loved Hannah, and I'm sure he didn't want her heart to be grieved, but he could not understand how with all that he blessed His wife with, how it did not make up for her being barren.

Elkanah may not have understood the deepest part of Hannah's pain, but God did. God understood even down to the place in prayer where Hannah's lips were moving but no words was coming out, because the spirit itself maketh intercession for us with groaning(s) which cannot be uttered (Romans 8:26b, KJV).

Family and friends will never understand our cry like God. Remember, God has put a limit on your love ones being able to understand and push you in your course with Him, because God wants to get the glory.

There is no limit, however, for you to push yourself with God's help. Right now, take a second and encourage yourself. And say, "No matter what, I have to keep travailing in prayer so my gifts and purpose can come forth."

Isaiah 66:8b says as soon as Zion travailed, she brought forth. "Before she travailed, she brought forth; before her pain came, she was delivered of a man child.[8] Who hath heard such a thing? who hath seen such things?" (Isaiah 66:7-8, KJV)

Therefore, based on Isaiah 66:7-8, when we travail in prayer, we can expect to see some results. In this Scripture, before Zion was advised to travail, a question was asked in verse 8. And I believe this question was asked to highlight the natural order to giving birth.

I thought about how usually when a person is ready to give birth to a child, the baby doesn't come first, and then the labor pains after. For naturally, the right order is to travail first, engage in laborious effort, then second come forth with a child.

Therefore, just like in the natural, so it is in the spiritual, the right order to coming forth in the gifts and purpose of God is to travail, and then we can expect to come forth with what God has formed in us.

As we think back on the story of Hannah, after the Scriptures said she was delivered from her barriers of bitterness and her sorrowful spirit, the Word follows up by saying, "God opened up her womb." God answered Hannah's prayer and granted her with a son and she called him Samuel. (1 Samuel 1:20) And this son Hannah gave birth to was a representation of Hannah, fulfilling her purpose.

For by Hannah giving birth to Samuel, after she travailed in prayer, this encourages me to be confident in knowing that when we travail, there will be a delivery. (Isaiah 66: 7-8)

Although God may not birth out everything He has formed in us at one time, we can be sure based on God's promise in Isaiah 66:7-8, there will be a deliverance and a birthing. (Isaiah 66:8b)

In 1 Samuel 1 and Isaiah 66:7-8, God's Word makes it clear— even in our season of affliction, as soon as we travail, as soon as we push with a fervent prayer, we can be delivered from the spirit of discouragement and every negative spirit that has attached itself, along with a blessing that will come forth. Tell yourself to never cease to fervently pray.

Push to be submissive to God's Word. How can you push yourself right now to be submissive to God's word?

Although saying a fervent prayer can be a way to encourage yourself, being submissive to God's Word is also another way.

Before Israel (Zion) was given the wisdom to travail, a prophet named Ezekiel had a vision of Israel being restored while he prophesied the Word of God. Ezekiel's vision came after Jerusalem had been destroyed. Israel had lost their temple and homes, and been taken from their land and placed in captivity in Babylon, because they had sinned with idolatry and disobedience to God. (2 Kings 25)

Ezekiel 37:1-3 is where the beginning of Ezekiel's vision is written: "The hand of the Lord was upon me, and carried me out in the spirit of the Lord, and set me down in the midst of the valley which was full of bones, And caused me to pass by them round about: and, behold, there were very many in the open valley; and, lo, they were very dry. And he said unto me, Son of man, can these bones live? And I answered, O Lord God, thou knows. (Ezekiel 37:1- 3, KJV)

Notice, Ezekiel's vision reveals two important matters. One, the people of Israel were in the valley (a low place in their spirits), and two, Ezekiel asked God an important question: Can these bones live? Ezekiel's question confirms that although the people of Israel were not physically dead, they were spiritually dead for not submitting to God, but the course of the world instead.

Ephesians 2:1-2, KJV – And you hath he quickened, who were dead in trespasses and sins; Wherein in time past ye walked according to the course of this world, according to the prince of the power of the air, the spirit that now worketh in the children of disobedience:

According to Ephesians 2:1-2, living in sin is to be spiritually dead in the eyes of God. Therefore, on the journey to fulfilling our purpose, we should be mindful that we can encounter situations that brings discouragement, because it's either a part of God's will or because of our action(s) of sin and disobedience.

Notice, when David encouraged himself with hope and Hannah prayed, David's discouragement happened because of the people's rage against David. And Hannah was discouraged because it was God's will that she encountered being barren. On the other hand, Israel was in a valley experience because of their sin and disobedience.

When we live in disobedience and sin, this will not only cause a delay in fulfilling our purpose in God, but also bondage and a separation from God, because God will not hear us. (Isaiah 59:2)

Isaiah 59:2, KJV – Your iniquities have separated between you and your God, and your sins have hidden his face from you, that he will not hear.

Although God has given many of us a calling and formed in us gifts and talents with a purpose, we were also born in sin. And not a day goes by that the flesh will not lust against the spirit and the spirit against the flesh: because these are contrary the one to the other, so that we cannot do the things that are pleasing unto God. (Galatians 5:17)

For it's the enemy's goal to persuade us not to submit to God, that we may fall into bondage and be totally disconnected from the Lord. Due to Satan being thrown out of heaven (Revelation 12:7-12), he tries everything he can to persuade us not to submit to God, that we may not receive the blessings of the Lord and fulfill our purpose in Him.

Despite Satan's efforts, God still holds each of us accountable for our actions of sin and disobedience. And relative to Isaiah 59:2, I personally don't want my sins to separate me from God nor His plan for my life.

As far as the sins of Israel, 2 Kings 17:7-20 is the Scripture that reveals the people of Israel's sin(s) and disobedience, and how such actions caused them to separate from God:

"For so it was, that the children of Israel had sinned against the Lord their God, which had brought them up out of the land of Egypt, from under the hand of Pharaoh king of Egypt, and had feared other God's, And walked in the statutes of the heathen, whom the Lord cast out from before the children of Israel, and of the kings of Israel, which they had made. And the children of Israel did secretly those things that were not right against the Lord their God, and they built them high places in all their cities, from the tower of the watchmen to the fenced city. And they set them up images and groves in every high hill, and under every green tree: And there they burnt incense in all the high places, as did the heathen whom the Lord carried away before them; and wrought wicked things to provoke the Lord to anger: For they served idols, whereof the Lord had said unto them, Ye shall not do this thing.

Yet the Lord testified against Israel, and against Judah, by all the prophets, and by all the seers, saying, Turn ye from your evil ways, and keep my commandments and my statutes, according to all the law which I commanded your fathers, and which I sent to you by my servants the prophets.

Notwithstanding they would not hear, but hardened their necks, like to the neck of their fathers, that did not believe in the Lord their God. And they rejected his statutes, and his covenant that he made with their fathers, and his testimonies which he testified against them; and they followed vanity, and became vain, and went after the heathen that were round about them, concerning whom the Lord had charged them, that they should not do like them.

And they left all the commandments of the Lord their God, and made them molten images, even two calves, and made a grove, and worshipped all the host of heaven, and served

Baal. And they caused their sons and their daughters to pass through the fire, and used divination and enchantments, and sold themselves to do evil in the sight of the Lord, to provoke him to anger. Therefore the Lord was very angry with Israel, and removed them out of his sight: there was none left but the tribe of Judah only.

Also Judah kept not the commandments of the Lord their God, but walked in the statutes of Israel which they made. And the Lord rejected all the seed of Israel, and afflicted them, and delivered them into the hand of spoilers, until he had cast them out of his sight." (KJV)

With God casting people of Israel out of his sight, because of their sin, this only causes me even more to push in submission to God's Word. Not only that I may please God, but to avoid having to encounter a season of unnecessary affliction and bondage as a consequence by God.

I imagine that had the people of Israel just submitted to God's Word and obeyed His commandment, the seventy years they spent in captivity could have perhaps been instead an experience of seventy years with favor, peace, and movement in God.

As far as myself personally, I remember times I didn't submit to God's Word, and by doing so, I wasted time that could have been used more wisely by following God instead. Because of my experience from not submitting to God, I now push each day to make an effort to submit to the word of God. I trust God and I don't want to delay any more time in my journey with Him due to actions of disobedience.

Because of Israel's lack of submission to God's Word, 2 Kings 17:7-18 confirms the people of Israel brought themselves into a place of bondage that led to a valley experience and disconnection from God.

God's commandments say, "Thou shall have no other God's before me." (Exodus 20:3, KJV) And God declares that obedience to His commandments is more important than offering sacrifices. (Jeremiah 7:21-28)

Clearly, even with what God declared in His word, Israel still disobeyed God. (2 Kings 17) And as a consequence, Israel was taken from their land, and brought into captivity. There was still hope for Israel because God promised they would be restored. God promised He would deliver them and restore the people of Israel back to Jerusalem. (Ezekiel 36:26 and Jeremiah 30:1-38:22)

Jeremiah 30:1-3,18-19, and 24 says:

*"This is the word that came to Jeremiah from the Lord:
This is what the Lord, the God of Israel, says: "Write in a
book all the words I have spoken to you. The days are
coming," declares the Lord, "when I will bring my people
Israel and Judah back from captivity and restore them to the
land I gave their ancestors to possess," says the Lord.'*

*This is what the Lord says: "I will restore the fortunes of
Jacob's tents and have compassion on his dwellings; the city
will be rebuilt on her ruins, and the palace will stand in its
proper place.*

*From them will come songs of thanksgiving and the sound of
rejoicing. I will add to their numbers, and they will not be
decreased;"*

I will bring them honor and they will not be disdained.

— 50 —

The fierce anger of the Lord will not turn back until he fully accomplishes the purposes of his heart. In days to come you will understand this."

These Scripture verses not only verify God's promise to restore the people of Israel, but I believe some of these verses reveal the heart of God to help those that are willing to push to submit to Him.

Ezekiel 36:26, KJV – A new heart also will I give you, and a new spirit will I put within you: and I will take away the stony heart out of your flesh, and I will give you a heart of flesh.

Being delivered from captivity and returning back to Jerusalem was an issue Israel needed help with. And God delivering Israel's heart of stone to a heart of flesh was an even bigger issue that God wanted to help change.

For a heart of stone versus a heart of flesh means a difference between unyielding to God's will and being sensitive to sin that will grieve the Lord.

Before Israel were released to go back to their land, God wanted them to have a heart that was submissive to His word and His will. By being submissive to God, songs of thanksgiving and rejoicing could be the outcome for the people of Israel, once they were delivered and restored.

God's way of how He dealt with Israel's captivity ensures us that although we may sin at times, and not yield to God, when we repent with sincere regret or remorse of our sins, this will create a new life and reconciliation with God. (2 Corinthians 5:17) For repentance will also allow God to shape and mold us into total submission to His word. And by submission, we can expect to be free and have the strength of God for our purpose in Him. (Psalm 16:11)

> *Acts 3:19, NIV – Repent, then, and turn to God, so that your sins may be wiped out, that times of refreshing may come from the Lord.*

God made a decree that Israel would repent and turn to Him —that He would cleanse Israel from all their sins and forgive them of rebellion. (Jeremiah 33:8) And He would be their God and they would be His people. (Jeremiah 30:22)

For this declaration of repentance and the promises of God to deliver and restore Israel were promises that were both good and kept.

God said, "So shall my word be that goeth forth out of my mouth: it shall not return unto me void, but it shall accomplish that which I please and it shall prosper. (Isaiah 55:11, KJV)

For although the promises of God's Word were guaranteed, Israel had to remain in captivity for seventy years before they could see the manifestation of God's promises. (Daniel 9:2) And the only way they could have made it through their valley experience was by standing on God's Word.

> *Push to stand on God's Word. How are you pushing yourself to stand on God's Word? How could you grow in that skill?*

During certain times, like Israel, we will have to wait on God to fulfill His promises. We may not have to wait seventy years, however the time that God does have us to wait, we may consider to be too long.

Therefore, while waiting on God, we must remain strong in faith and in His will, and we should strive to stand on the Word of God.

For while the people of Israel were in captivity waiting on the promises of God, God gave Ezekiel an instruction that required him to prophesy—meaning to state the divine will of the word of the Lord.

> *Ezekiel 37:4-6, KJV – Then he said to me, "Prophesy over these bones, and say to them, O dry bones, hear the word of the Lord. Thus says the Lord God to these bones: Behold, I will cause breath to enter you, and you shall live. And I will lay sinews upon you, and will cause flesh to come upon you, and cover you with skin, and put breath in you, and you shall live, and you shall know that I am the Lord.*

Romans 10:17 says, "So then faith cometh by hearing, and hearing by the word of God." (KJV) When God told Ezekiel to prophesy the Word of God, I gathered God was subliminally saying, *Remind Israel of the promises of my Word (I first gave through Jeremiah), so that their faith will be charged.*

Based on Romans 10:17, when Ezekiel spoke God's word, I imagine this not only sharpened the focus of faith into the ear gate of Israel, but eliminated the distraction of them being in a low place.

Researchers have written a theory that when words are spoken, it is effectively good for us. Whether you are speaking the Word of God, instructions on putting an item together, or words from a song, saying words out loud sharpens our focus and eliminates distractions.[2]

---

[2] literaturelust.com/Melissa gouty

Hearing the Word of God and then standing on the Word of God, will encourage us while being in a hard place and encountering a season of affliction. For the power of God's Word has the strength to help us make it, even while on broken pieces.

As Ezekiel prophesied the Word of God in his vision, God was showing the life of the people of Israel being slowly restored.

> *Ezekiel 37:7-10, KJV – So I prophesied as I was commanded: and as I prophesied, there was a noise, and behold a shaking, and the bones came together, bone to his bone. And when I beheld, lo, the sinews and the flesh came up upon them, and the skin covered them above: but there was no breath in them. Then said he unto me, Prophesy unto the wind, prophesy, son of man, and say to the wind, Thus saith the Lord God; Come from the four winds, O breath, and breathe upon these slain, that they may live. So I prophesied as he commanded me, and the breath came into them, and they lived, and stood up upon their feet, an exceeding great army.*

In Ezekiel's vision, before breath came into Israel and before they stood on their feet, notice there were stages of restoration that took place. (Ezekiel 37:7-10) And due to these stages, I believe God was revealing that sometimes, for Him to completely deliver and restore us, it may take more than one breakthrough.

For while God's Word is being spoken into our ear, it opens a gate to release faith and life. The spirit of the enemy is also on his post, trying to prevent the spirit of darkness, disobedience, and discouragement, from being broken and defeated. (John 10:10)

Nevertheless, the power of God's Word will always prevail. For God's Word is quick, and powerful, and sharper than any two-edged sword, piercing even to the dividing asunder of soul and spirit, and of the joints and marrow. (Hebrews 4:12)

And based on Hebrews 4:12, in Ezekiel's vision, when the valley of dry bones was restored to the life of a strong human-being, this showed God's Word to be true and powerful. However, although God's Word was powerful to restore Israel's spirit, Israel still had another breakthrough to wait on, which was returning to their land. Therefore, another round of hearing God's word was needed.

> ***Ephesians 37:12-14, KJV*** *– Therefore prophesy and say unto them, Thus saith the Lord God; Behold, O my people, I will open your graves, and cause you to come up out of your graves, and bring you into the land of Israel. And ye shall know that I am the Lord, when I have opened your graves, O my people, and brought you up out of your graves, And shall put my spirit in you, and ye shall live, and I shall place you in your own land: then shall ye know that I the Lord have spoken it, and performed it, saith the Lord.*

Based on what God says in these verses (Ephesians 37:12-14), it gives hope to the people of Israel that what God has promised in Jeremiah 30:1-38:22 is still coming to pass.

For just as God has confirmed through Ezekiel's vision that what He said will be for the people of Israel, this should ensure you that what God said concerning your life shall be also. For whatsoever God has promised you personally and within His word, tell yourself "It's still coming to pass."

Ezekiel's vision gave one of the best sources to use to overcome any encounter that brings discouragement in our journey to fulfilling our purpose. And it's the Word of God. No matter what some days may feel like, or look like we can trust God's Word. For God is not a man that shall lie. (Numbers 23:19)

In Ezra 1:1-4,11 it shows that God kept his promise. After seventy years of captivity, the people of Israel were able to return back to their land and rebuild. A King of Persia, named Ezra, (who was given all the kingdoms of the earth), makes an announcement instructed by God to go back to Jerusalem and build a temple of the Lord for the God of Israel.

Ezra 1:1-4,11 (KJV) says:

Ezra 1:1-4,11 KJV – Now in the first year of Cyrus king of Persia, that the Word of the Lord by the mouth of Jeremiah might be fulfilled, the Lord stirred up the spirit of Cyrus king of Persia, that he made a proclamation throughout all his kingdom, and also put in writing, saying

Thus saith Cyrus king of Persia, The Lord God of heaven hath given me all the kingdoms of the earth; and he hath charged me to build him an house at Jerusalem, which is in Judah

Who is there among you of all his people? his God be with him, and let him go up to Jerusalem, which is in Judah, and build the house of the Lord God of Israel, (he is the God,) which is in Jerusalem.

And whosoever remained in any place where he sojourneth, let the men of his place help him with silver, and with gold, and with goods, and with beasts, beside the freewill offering for the house of God that is in Jerusalem

— 56 —

All the vessels of gold and of silver were five thousand and four hundred. All these did Sheshbazzar (prince of Judah) bring up with them of the captivity that were brought up from Babylon unto Jerusalem.

These verses in Ezra 1 not only prove God kept His promise to the people of Israel , but when God delivers and fulfills his promise to us, a heart of worship unto him is God's desire. For the outcome of restoration that God gave Israel after their valley experience shows we may fall in sin, encounter painful times, and have to wait on God for a breakthrough, but God who is our redeemer, strong tower and keeper of His word will show up.

For what God has for you is greater than your struggle and difficult times. Therefore, don't give up, but continue to push yourself towards the mark of your high calling in Christ Jesus. (Philippians 3:14)

Now, decree and declare: "I am a midwife and no matter what; I will not let my seed of greatness die, but live."

5

The Development to Flourish

Psalm 92:12, KJV – The righteous shall flourish like the palm tree: he shall grow like a cedar in Lebanon.

The most common growth developments that humans share are the stages from being a new born, to an adolescent, to a teenager, and then to an adult. However, although humans share these natural growth stages, spiritual development and maturity is not something we all have in common. Not everyone practices the same religion or has the same faith in God.

Now, although there are numerous people in the world that have decided to believe in God, the desire to grow into a spiritual life of righteousness in God may not be the same case. Going to church services and doing a good deed here and there is the only way many desire to live relative to Christianity. But going the extra mile and living a life of righteousness according to God's Word is the only way to flourish in all the blessings God has planned for the righteous believer.

Psalm 92:12 states the righteous shall flourish—which is a good, expected promise to hold on to. However, it's important to know who God calls the righteous. For there certainly is a difference between who the world considers to be righteous and who is called righteous in the eyes of God.

For people may argue the righteous are those that show acts of kindness, do good deeds, or wear styles of clothing that look holy. And surely, giving money to the poor, food to the hungry, and giving donations to a good cause, or even helping someone in need are all honorable acts.

However, when we look at God's Word, the kingdom of heaven calls the righteous, people that have been justified by faith, meaning in transition from sin to right-relationship with God:

> *Philippians 3:9, NIV – And be found in him not having a righteous of my own that comes from the law, but that which is through faith in Christ, the righteousness that comes from God on the basis of faith.*

In this Scripture, notice what is said and what isn't. The perspective that the righteous are persons with perfect holiness apparel or good behavioral acts are not written in this verse. But what is written, is that the righteousness that comes from God is on the basis of faith.

Therefore, those that deem the righteous to be based on moral standards and keeping the laws of the land is not whom God is speaking of. And without repentance of sin and faith in God, the righteousness of God's will cannot be done.

> *Galatians 5:4, KJV – And Christ is become of no effect unto you whosever of you are justified by the law; ye are fallen from grace.*

In the eyes of God, faith sets the foundation to be called righteous in the kingdom of God. And all can be justified freely without their own works and merits, by grace, through the redemption, that's with in the blood of Jesus. (Romans 3:23-25)

The Righteous Shall Flourish

Once justified by faith and called righteous by God.

Then the promise of Psalm 92:12, "to flourish, will be thy portion." Now, let me define what it means to flourish by the Merriam dictionary versus God's meaning.

The dictionary defines the meaning to flourish this way, "To grow or develop in a healthy favorable way, and to achieve success, in a state of activity or production, reaching a height of development and or influence. (Merriam Dictionary)

Naturally, when anyone puts in the work required to grow or make an achievement, he or she will see the results of their consistency and time. For there is no secret, if you work hard, you will see the fruit of your labor.

However, just like there is a difference in who God calls righteous, there also is a special way that God will have the righteous of God to flourish.

The Righteous Shall Flourish Like a Palm Tree

Psalm 92:12 says, "The righteous shall flourish like the palm tree: he shall grow like a cedar in Lebanon." (KJV)

In the first part of Psalm 92:12 notice the righteous shall flourish like a palm tree. Palm trees are special unlike any other type of tree.

Hallett Taylor wrote an article on some fascinating facts about palm trees, stating:[3]

1. A palm is a symbol of life.
2. Palm trees can reach heights of 70ft or much more.

Each fact is a good representation of exactly the way God says He will flourish the righteous.

For Taylor's fact of a palm tree being a "symbol of life" means living a life beyond existence. And although the literal meaning of "life" is the existence of an individual, human being, or animal, when we search deeper beyond this definition, and focus on the symbol of life relative to a palm tree, I believe a deeper look reveals how a palm tree of life means more than just existing on earth.

Even without having the knowledge of what a palm tree symbolizes, many people would already agree that life is beyond existing. However, the idea of what gives a person life beyond existing may result in several different perspectives.

The majority of people in this world think that the main portal that gives a person life (in addition to the air that is breathe) is achieving and reaching major points of success. And I also believe that many in the world define these points of success to be based on the list below:

1. Achieving the American Dream
2. Buying a house

[3] the spruce.com

— 61 —

3. Earning a six figure or greater income
4. Owning luxury cars
5. having a business owned development(s)
6. Obtaining the highest level of education
7. Finding the right soul mate
8. Having a Provision of materialistic things.

For once a person obtains some and or all the goals that I listed above, think about it—does reaching these achievements and success of things truly give a person life? What truly gives life is following after the righteousness and the mercy of God.

Proverbs 21:21, KJV – He that followed after righteousness and mercy findeth life, righteousness, and honor.

For regardless of all the wealth that a person obtains, wealth is worthless in the day of wrath, but righteousness delivers from death. (Proverbs 11:4) In other words, we may exist on earth and achieve the wealth of the land, and even many levels of success. However, when judgement day comes from God, our possessions and achievements won't be able to save us from death. For the unrighteous will not only lose their wealth and possessions, but will also lose having eternal life in heaven.

Based on Psalm 92:12 and the knowledge of a palm tree representing a symbol of life, we can be ensured the righteous will not only grow in life on earth, but eternal life shall be what the righteous flourish to. Tell yourself, "What truly gives life is living through Jesus Christ."

John 11:25-26, MSG – You don't have to wait for the End. I am, right now, Resurrection and Life. The one who believes in me, even though he or she dies, will live.

God's word makes it clear—those that choose life through Jesus Christ are not only called righteous, but will live and not die. (Psalm 118:17) For we were created with an opportunity to have eternal life. And if your declaration is to live for Christ, then tell yourself to get ready to flourish beyond what you can see right now.

Flourish Beyond What's Average

Once we have repented and God calls us "righteous", we not only are guaranteed, according to God's word to have eternal life, but while we are living on earth, we can live beyond a life that is average. In other words, we can live a life which enables us to experience all of the prosperity God has in store for us, while carrying out our assignment(s) given by God.

> *Deuteronomy 28:13, NKJV – The LORD will make you the head and not the tail; you shall be above only, and not be beneath, if you heed the commandments of the LORD your God, which I command you today, and are careful to observe them.*

Relative to Deuteronomy 28:13, the second fact listed about palm trees symbolizes flourishing beyond an average point. In fact, palm trees are able to reach heights of 70ft or much more. Which can mean, based on both this fact about palm trees and Psalm 92:12, the righteous are capable of growing beyond levels that are considered average in areas of both the natural and spiritual. But in order to flourish beyond the point of what's ordinary, obeying God is a must. And pushing passed both fear and your comfort zone is also necessary.

Push Passed Fear

Although God has given us a promise in Psalm 92:12 that the righteous will flourish like a palm tree, God didn't say that we would flourish without labor.

Therefore, once God has affirmed your assignment and or calling, it's imperative to not only push to give birth to your purpose, but to push to flourish in what God has given you to do. And while pushing, tell yourself, "Don't forget about the enemy's devices."

For just like the enemy doesn't want you to come forth in your purpose, the enemy also doesn't want you to flourish in your purpose. And many times, one of the devices the enemy uses as a way of preventing growth and prosperity in God is through the spirit of fear.

> *2 Timothy 1:7, KJV* – *For God has not given us a spirit of fear, but of power and of love and of a sound mind.*

The fact that Timothy says God has not given us the spirit of fear verifies that if fear is not from God, then the enemy plays a part in the torment that fear gives.

In Joshua chapter 1, Joshua a minister and successor to Moses, shows that we can push passed both the spirit of fear and our comfort zone to fulfill an assignment given by God.

Joshua 1:1-7 tells of Joshua's assignment that led both Joshua and the children of Israel to flourish:

> *Joshua 1:1-7, KJV* – *Now after the death of Moses the servant of the Lord it came to pass, that the lord spake unto Joshua the son of Nun, Moses' minister, saying, Moses my servant is dead; now therefore arise, go over this Jordan, thou, and all this people, unto the land which I do give to them,*

even to the children of Israel. Every place that the sole of
your foot shall tread upon, that have I given unto you, as I
said unto Moses. From the wilderness and this Lebanon even
unto the great river, the river Euphrates, all the land of the
Hittites, and unto the great sea toward the going down of the
sun, shall be your coast. There shall not any man be able to
stand before thee all the days of thy life: as I was with
Moses, so I will be with thee: I will not fail thee, nor forsake
thee. Be strong and of a good courage: for unto this people
shalt thou divide for an inheritance the land, which I swore
unto their fathers to give them. Only be thou strong and very
courageous, that thou mayest observe to do according to all the
law, which Moses my servant commanded thee: turn not from
it to the right hand or to the left, that thou mayest prosper
withersoever thou guest. This book of the law shall not
depart out of thy mouth; but thou shalt meditate therein day
and night, that thou mayest observe to do according to all that
is written therein: for then thou shalt make thy way
prosperous, and then thou shalt have good success. Have not I
commanded thee? Be strong and of a good courage; be not
afraid, neither be thou dismayed: for the Lord thy God is
with thee whithersoever thou guest.

"Be not afraid and be of good courage." Notice that this is the main command that God gave Joshua after giving him his assignment to lead Israel into the promise land. And the idea that God told Joshua not to be afraid and courageous three times, I gather, is because Joshua was severely gripped with fear.

However, God tells Joshua in Joshua 1:8, In order to make thy way prosperous and have good success, Joshua had to speak, meditate, observe, and do what God said. In other words, in order for Joshua to flourish, he had to be courageous in carrying out the instructions that God gave him.

In addition to this, God assured Joshua that He would be with him. (Joshua 1:5) In Matthew 28:20, God tells us similar words, that He is with us always even unto the end of the world.

And Based on Matthew 28:20, we can find comfort and strength in knowing that with God with us, we have the help we need to push passed fear and be courageous in doing what God has assigned us to do.

What fear do you need to push passed to show courage today?

Although we can stand on Matthew 28:20, during certain times we will wrestle with the fear of carrying out the assignment God has given us to do. For the enemy will be consistent in trying to frighten us through negative thoughts and emotions of what could possibly go wrong in our task. However, despite the enemy's tactics, it's imperative to stand strong in taking on courage and moving with the ability to do God's will, even while frightened.

For, there were many times in the course of my journey in God where I needed courage. However, now, whenever I am afraid, I encourage myself to look at the bigger picture, to decide would I rather let my fears stop me from flourishing to my maximum potential, or do I work my purpose scared and believe that God has me in every step and won't let me be ashamed.

For I also stand on 1 Corinthians 2:9 which also gives encouragement to be courageous:

1 Corinthians 2:9, KJV – But as it is written, Eye hath not seen, nor ear heard, neither have entered into the heart of man, the things which God hath prepared for them, that love God.

I love this Scripture of inspiration, because it gives me a vision that the level I'm on now is not the final level that God has predestined for me. Thank God, because of my vision of growing to a greater level in Him, I chose each day to follow God's instructions. And for every time that I chose to overcome fear, and carry out my God given assignment, God has proven Himself to be faithful in blessing me. Some blessings were tangible, and other blessings were of strength, growth, favor, deliverance, and healing. And other blessings were based on open doors that brought me closer to flourishing in my purpose in God.

Therefore, because of the results of me being courageous, I know for myself it's better to do God's will scared than to let fear be a hinderance. And I challenge you to also be courageous in doing what God has assigned you. (1 Corinthians 2:9, Translation)

In Joshua 1:10-11, it shows that Joshua decided to be of good courage, for Joshua commanded the children of Israel, to set out to do what God assigned:

Joshua 1:11 KJV – Then Joshua commanded the officers of the people, saying, Pass through the host, and command the people, saying, Prepare you victuals; for within three days ye shall pass over this Jordan, to go in to possess the land, which the Lord your God giveth you to possess it.

By Joshua taking on the courage to possess the promised land, this overcame the first hurdle of fear to begin his assignment. However, there were two more hurdles to overcome. For one, Israel had to deal with the Jordan river overflowing its banks with no boats to across Jordan. And second, Israel had to deal with the strong, tall walls of Jericho, that was between them and the promised land. (Joshua 6:1-20)

Based on these two obstacles, this all could have been enough for Joshua to reconsider fulfilling His assignment. After all, when God told Joshua to be courageous in Joshua 1: 1-7, God didn't mention at the same time all the details required to possess the land. All God basically said was, Do what my law says and then thy way would be prosperous. Therefore, based on the partial details Joshua received, for him to have completed his assignment, he had to also push passed his comfort zone.

Push passed your comfort zone. Where are you staying in your comfort zone right now?

Similar to Joshua, when God gives an assignment, notice He never gives you all the details at once. And being we are only given details in parts (1 Corinthians 13:9), there have been a few times that after I said yes, Lord, in the process of doing my assignment, I started to have second thoughts. In this case, it wasn't because I was afraid, but I was thinking that perhaps what's required is too uncomfortable and would take me outside of my comfort zone. But in time, I made an ultimate decision to push passed what I gathered to be my places of comfort.

The places or situations you feel safe, or at ease, or without stress are your comfort zones. If you use this meaning relative to your relationship with God, your gifts, and the assignments that God has given you for His kingdom, it will help you realize if you're operating inside or outside of your comfort zone.

For example, just going to church on Sunday or occasionally serving on a ministry team is easy to handle. Saying a daily, quick prayer and reading one Scripture verse a day are also examples of what a comfortable place in God looks like. There is nothing wrong with these actions and tasks—they're all good. But the downfall of these examples is, they represent doing what's easy and convenient in the things of God. Which only results in not flourishing to the same level as a person that pushes passed their comfort zone.

I believe in relation to our assignment(s) given by God, pushing each day to follow God's instructions, regardless of the assignment, and going the extra mile takes submission to God and operating outside of a comfort zone.

When God gave Joshua the instructions on how to cross over the Jordan river, the course of orders were not easy:

> ***Joshua 3:3-8, NIV*** *– After three days the officers went throughout the camp, giving orders to the people: "When you see the ark of the covenant of the Lord your God, and the Levitical priests carrying it, you are to move out from your positions and follow it. Then you will know which way to go, since you have never been this way before. But keep a distance of about two thousand cubits between you and the ark; do not go near it."*
>
> *Joshua told the people, "Consecrate yourselves, for tomorrow the Lord will do amazing things among you." Joshua said to the priests, "Take up the ark of the covenant and pass on ahead of the people." So, they took it up and went ahead of them.*

*And the Lord said to Joshua, "Today I will begin to exalt
you in the eyes of all Israel, so they may know that I am
with you as I was with Moses. Tell the priests who carry the
ark of the covenant: 'When you reach the edge of the
Jordan's waters, go and stand in the river.'"*

These instructions were not easy and or convenient to carry
out. Therefore, this leaves me to believe that both Joshua and
Israel actually did operate outside of their comfort zone.

The orders given to Israel, based on fasting, following the
Ten Commandments, and standing flat footed in the Jordan
River were not only about crossing the Jordan, but also a
representation of these three points:

1. A development to flourish
2. Total submission to an assignment for God's will
3. Enduring a course of inconvenience

And with both Joshua and Israel choosing to carry out the
instructions that God gave them, God performed a miracle.
A miracle which included crossing over the Jordan River on
dry ground, and a miracle representing a step closer to
entering into a place that would enable Joshua and Israel to
live beyond average.

We find the details of this miracle in Joshua:

*Joshua 3:14-17, NIV – So, when the people broke camp
to cross the Jordan, the priests carrying the ark of the
covenant went ahead of them.*

*Now the Jordan is at flood stage all during harvest. Yet as
soon as the priests who carried the ark reached the Jordan
and their feet touched the water's edge,*

*the water from upstream stopped flowing. It piled up in a
heap a great distance away, at a town called Adam in the
vicinity of Zarethan, while the water flowing down to the Sea
of the Arabah (that is, the Dead Sea) was completely cut off.
So, the people crossed over opposite Jericho.*

*The priests who carried the ark of the covenant of the Lord
stopped in the middle of the Jordan and stood on dry ground,
while all Israel passed by until the whole nation had
completed the crossing on dry ground." (NIV)*

This miracle proves, whenever a believer is obedient and operates outside of their comfort zone for the purpose of God's will, God will do whatever he has to do to put that believer on a route that will enable him or her to flourish . And because this miracle did bring Joshua and Israel closer to the promise land, I imagine this also encouraged Joshua to continue to be courageous and push passed his comfort zone as he continued to move on in his assignment.

Similar to Joshua, whenever we are operating in an assignment given by God, another way that can help keep us with a courageous attitude and moving outside of our comfort zone is by remembering the victories that were already won through Christ.

When I remind myself of the hurdles that God has helped me cross over while doing His will, it reassures me that God will also help me overcome the hurdles that I'm faced with along the way in my journey.

Just as God helped both Joshua and Israel overcome the hurdle to cross over the Jordan River, God surely did help Israel overcome the wall of Jericho. Joshua 6:1-27)

In Joshua 6: 15-16, & 20 is listed the last steps that Joshua and Israel accomplished before seeing the wall of Jericho come down:

> *Joshua 6:15-16, 20, NIV – On the seventh day, they got up at daybreak and marched around the city seven times in the same manner, except that on that day they circled the city seven times. The seventh time around, when the priests sounded the trumpet blast, Joshua commanded the army, "Shout! For the Lord has given you the city!"*
>
> *When the trumpets sounded, the army shouted, and at the sound of the trumpet, when the men gave a loud shout, the wall collapsed; so, everyone charged straight in, and they took the city.*

Both Joshua and the children of Israel had another victory. Again, their obedience to God's instructions (signifying their courage), and their press to push passed their comfort zone enabled them to take the city of Jericho and enter into the promised land called Canaan, a land flowing with milk and honey (Numbers 14:8), signifying a place where there was plenty of food, money, and life was good.

In other words, both Joshua and Israel flourished into a place above average. And because Joshua was the leader that lead Israel into the promised land, Joshua also flourished in his assignment.

Flourish in your assignment. What is one assignment God has given you in life right now? Are you flourishing in it?

In Joshua 1:1-9, we recognize that the assignment that God gave Joshua was not only for him to benefit from, but also for the children of Israel. If Joshua would have allowed his comfort zone and the spirit of fear to hinder him, he would have aborted his assignment and missed out on God's plan, for both him and the children of Israel to flourish in Canaan together.

Similar to Joshua, the assignments that God has given you are needed to help someone else flourish. Imagine— with you carrying out your assignment, being courageous, and moving outside of your comfort zone, how it could save your loved ones, a family member, or a stranger from losing out on the life that Christ has for them to receive. And with you submitting to help someone else grow in the righteousness and purpose of God, in return, you will also flourish and be abundantly blessed.

> ***Proverbs 11:25, NKJV*** *– The generous soul will be made rich, and he who waters will also be watered himself.*

Esther 3-10 verifies that when you help someone else within God's plan, blessings happen for you and the person you help.

Notice, in the book of Esther, the two people that flourish are Esther, who became a queen by marrying King Ahasuerus, and her cousin Mordecai, who worked outside the gate of the king's palace.

However, before Esther and Mordecai reached their point of flourishing, Esther 3:5 says that Mordecai was threatened to be killed because he refused to bow down to man, the king's chief advisor. Furthermore, with Mordecai's refusal to bow, Haman used his authority to set a plot to have Mordecai and all the other Jews killed.

Recognize, by Mordecai's refusal to bow down to Haman and only to God, this showed an action I believe that represented courage and a message that no matter what the enemy says and or tries to do, stand for what you know is right and for what you believe.

Therefore, with Mordecai's courage not to bow to Haman, this did not cause any danger for Esther's life, because neither did the king nor Haman know that Esther was a Jew. However, Esther did what she could do to help Mordecai and the other Jews from being killed by Haman's plot.

Esther helped by setting up a plan to pray and fast for three days, and then, to convince the king to stop the scheduled killing of both Mordecai and the other Jews.

And with Esther's burden to both pray and fast, to prevent Mordecai and the Jews from being killed, Esther's purpose was revealed. It was not only about being a queen in a palace, but she had an assignment by God to save the Jews.

Although Esther was not a leader like Joshua, who lead others to the promised land, Esther's prayers and fasting were just as effective in helping others come out of a place of distress.

Sometimes, the only way God will use us to help someone else is by praying or fasting.

1 Corinthians 3:6 basically says that some plant, some water, and God gives the increase: "And he who plants and he who waters are one, and each one will receive his own reward according to his labor (1 Corinthians 3:8, NKJV).

In other words, we can only help someone else with the ability and way that God has assigned us, because ultimately God is the only One that can open up the way for us to be blessed and to flourish. However, for the level at which we allow God to use us, we will be rewarded.

Therefore, with Mordecai's stand for God and Esther's plan to pray and fast, God began to work it out for Mordecai and the Jews to prevail over Haman's plot of death.

God changed the heart of King Ahasuerus, which lead to the king cancelling Haman's plan to kill the Jews and the king commanding for Haman to be killed instead. Even more, Mordecai was kept alive and promoted from being a gatekeeper to the position that Haman had, as the chief advisor to the king.

As you see, God's hand operated throughout this entire situation from beginning to end. God blessed Mordecai with victory, plus an elevation because of his courage to stand for God. And Esther remained with the favor of God Because she helped saved her Jewish people from death. Tell yourself, "I need to push somebody else to flourish."

Based on Psalm 92:12, and the books of both Joshua and Esther, God's Word verifies that the righteous will be ultimately bless by carrying out their assignment by God. However, only God knows the timing of when He chooses to flourish man for carrying out their assignments.

I believe that sometimes we may flourish immediately after doing a task by God, and other times, we will have to wait on God. Therefore, while you're in your development to flourish, I encourage you to stay strong.

Now, stay strong. How do you need to show strength right now?

For the Scripture used for the foundation of this chapter was based on the "a clause" of Psalm 92:12, that says the righteous shall flourish like the palm tree, and the second part (b clause) of this scripture says, "he shall grow like a cedar in Lebanon." (KJV)

Cedar trees symbolize strength. Therefore, based on both this study and Psalm 92:12 (b clause), this can assure that God has equipped the righteous to be strong in Him. However, it's up to the righteous to embrace the strength that God gives to grow strong.

> ***Galatians 6:9, KJV*** *– And let us not be weary in well doing: for in due season we shall reap, if we faint not.*

Galatians 6:9 (a clause) inspires, to not undergo spiritual maturity with a posture of weariness, but to stand on the Word of God that assures you will be rewarded at the right time for doing what you been assigned by God to do.

Many trials will come in our journey with God that will test our willingness to accomplish what God has called and assigned us to do. However, the fact that Psalm 92:12 (b clause) says that God is willing to grow us like a cedar in Lebanon also shows that God not only intends for us to be strong, but God intends us for to make it to our destiny in Him.

Therefore, don't give up. Be encouraged to keep growing to the capacity that God has for you to flourish. And use the dominion God has authorized you to used to stay strong in doing the work of the Lord, and also in reaching your destiny in Christ Jesus. (Ephesians 2:8-10)

Now, decree and declare I am a midwife and no matter what;
I will not let my seed of greatness die, but live.

6

Believe

Romans 15:13, KJV – Now the God of hope fill you with all joy and peace in believing, that ye may abound in hope, through the power of the Holy Ghost.

The assignment, gift, ability, or plan that God has given you can be summed up in this one word, called "greatness". Greatness is defined as the quality of being important and skilled in doing or using something. (Oxford Dictionary) Furthermore, as the greatness God has formed in you comes forth, there's one major substance to incorporate at all times in your journey, "believe".

Merriam Dictionary says to believe means to have a firm conviction as to the goodness, efficacy (the power to produce an effect), or ability of something. For this definition can be used in reference to believing in God, people, places, things, and even in relation to believing in yourself.

Believe in yourself. Do you believe in yourself? Why or why not?

I believe the motivation needed to accomplish anything in life should start and end with having self-confidence—a feeling of trust in one's abilities, qualities, and judgment (Dictionary).

For if you can believe in yourself, then that's half the battle won.

For instance, there is a movie that came out in 2020 that aired on Netflix, called, "Jingle Jangle: A Christmas Journey", written by David E. Talbert, with a message about believing in yourself.

The movie is about a toy inventor who owned his own invention business. His creativity at one time brought hope for his family, a lot of customers, and much profit. Until one day, an inside employee stole his inventions, leaving this owner broken-hearted, without hope, and without confidence that he could ever create another toy invention that would be special or even bring in the money he needed.

However, once this inventor chose to believe again, that's when the joy and peace of life was restored to him. When he believed, he was able to put together a toy invention that brought the hope, income, and love needed to restore his gift of creativity and his business and family.

The message from this movie is very profound—believe and believe in yourself. And just as important as it was for the toy inventor to believe, it's important for you to believe in the greatness that's to be birthed out of you. You can't be effective in being a midwife for the purpose of God and not believe in what God has formed in you.

Now, I'm aware that believing in oneself is not as easy as said, because no one is actually born with self-assurance. Self-confidence is a quality that has to be developed. Denis Waitley puts it this way, "No one is born with self-confidence, self-confidence is learned and earned with experience."

However, in any case when someone struggles with self-confidence, either because of a negative upbringing, so-called friends, or the experience of unhealthy relationships, through Jesus Christ, there is healing, deliverance and the hope that one needs to believe in oneself and move on without self-doubt in their journey to giving birth to greatness.

Mark 9:24 says, "And straightway, the father of the child cried out, and said with tears, Lord, I believe; help thou mine unbelief." (KJV) This plea, shows the reality for many. For several reasons, insecurity and uncertainty can be our road block to destiny. However, when we cry out to God in times of uncertainty, God can help one's unbelief.

In Mark 9:24, the father wanted his sick son to be healed. And because Jesus told him that he would need to believe, the father's response in asking Jesus to help him believe, demonstrated the father's passion for deliverance from doubt.

Believe in who God created you to be. Who did God create you to be?

Mark 9:24 assures that the Lord can help our unbelief, therefore no one ought to tolerate living with lack of confidence, regardless of what caused it. "For ye are a chosen generation, a royal priesthood, an holy nation, a peculiar people; that ye should show forth the praises of him who hath called you out of darkness into his marvelous light." (1 Peter 2:9, KJV)

The enemy each day will challenge you on what the Word of God says about you. Satan loves to kill our self-confidence, not cockiness nor arrogance, but rather a made-up mind that says I believe in who God says that I am.

For with the right confident mindset, attacks from the enemy will come at times through people you least expect. However, I've learned to stay ahead of the enemy's plot, to simply pray, "Lord, deliver me from people. And Lord, help me to stay focused on who you say that I am, and not the negative opinions of man."

For David said it best, "Though an army besiege me my heart will not fear, though war break against me, even then I will be confident." (Psalm 27:3, KJV)

God has already put His stamp of approval on who you are in Him. All you have to do is believe it for yourself, regardless of who else doesn't believe in you. If God formed the gift, talent, and call in you, then God has qualified you to use it and walk powerfully and successfully in it.

Psalm 139:13-14, NIV – For you created my inmost being; you knit me together in my mother's womb. I praise you because I am fearfully and wonderfully made; your works are wonderful, I know that full well.

This chapter of Psalm 139 confirms that God has created man to be wonderful, to be a force to be reckoned with. However, before David speaks of being fearfully and wonderfully made, he mentions in Psalm 139:1 & 3 that God has searched him and has "compassest" his path and that the Lord is acquainted with all of his ways.

Furthermore, for David to begin with this information, this shows that David recognized that though he was created to be wonderful, he also was born with imperfections. But even with his imperfections, God still saw his substance. In other words, God saw his distinctive qualities. Psalm 139:16 (a clause) says, "Thine eyes did see my substance, yet being unperfect." (KJV)

Trust your substance. Do you trust your substance?

Because of the love of God, even though we were born in sin (Psalm 51:5), God wants us to be certain about the substance that we were also born with.

"Certainly if we say that we have no sin we deceive ourselves and the truth is not in us." (1 John 1:8, KJV). But when we examine ourselves, by being honest in admitting our weaknesses and faults in God's presence, God, in return, can give us the confidence we need to believe that, while being delivered from sin, He is able to use His plan through us, with the wonderful and mighty works God formed in us.

Only Satan wants you to focus on your imperfections, so you won't be mindful of coming forth with your substance. "Therefore, submit to God. Resist the devil and he will flee from you." (James 4:7, NKJV).

Satan is a liar. You can be great through Christ, even with your flaws.

King David is a fine example of a person that God used mightily, even with imperfections. In chapter three of this book, I mentioned the strengths that David had shown before he was officially made the king of Israel.

Now, notice in 2 Samuel 11 David's weaknesses as a ruling king:

> *2 Samuel 11:3-6, KJV – And David sent and enquired after the woman. And one said, Is not this Bathsheba, the daughter of Eliam, the wife of Uriah the Hittite? And*

David sent messengers, and took her; and she came in unto him, and he lay with her; for she was purified from her uncleanness: and she returned unto her house. And the woman conceived, and sent and told David, and said, I am with child And David sent to Joab, saying, Send me Uriah the Hittite. And Joab sent Uriah to David.

2 Samuel 11:14-17, KJV – And it came to pass in the morning, that David wrote a letter to Joab, and sent it by the hand of Uriah. And he wrote in the letter, saying, Set ye Uriah in the forefront of the hottest battle, and retire ye from him, that he may be smitten, and die. And it came to pass, when Joab observed the city, that he assigned Uriah unto a place where he knew that valiant men were. And the men of the city went out, and fought with Joab: and there fell some of the people of the servants of David; and Uriah the Hittite died also.

When David first became king, the actions he showed relative to these Scriptures exposes David's imperfections—adultery with a married woman who became pregnant with his child.

However, perhaps David's biggest flaw is shown when David plotted to kill Bathsheba's husband, Uriah.

However, even with God knowing that David would commit adultery and plan a murder, recognize that God still predestined for David to be king and a man after God's own heart. (1 Samuel 13:14)

Furthermore, aside from David, In Acts 9:1-5, there is another man with imperfections. In spite of his flaws, God saw his substance:

Acts 9:1-2, KJV – And Saul, yet breathing out threatenings and slaughter against the disciples of the Lord, went unto the high priest, And desired of him letters to Damascus to the synagogues, that if he found any of this way, whether they were men or women, he might bring them bound unto Jerusalem.

Based on these two verses, the actions of Saul threatening anyone that followed Christ was his imperfection. However, while Saul was on his way to a place called Damascus to arrest men and women in Christ, things changed.

Saul had an encounter with God, and by this experience, Saul's heart was changed days later. For this God-encounter changed Saul's name to Paul and changed his efforts from being a persecutor of the disciples of Christ, to instead a witness and preacher for the son of God. (Acts 9:20)

For although the imperfection of Paul (Saul) was persecuting anyone that followed the way of Christ, the substance that God saw in him was that he was destined to be a preacher to win souls for the kingdom of God. (Acts 9:20)

As you see through God's Word, even in our imperfections God still sees our substance, therefore we ought to see our substance as well. For your imperfections may not be of such like David or Paul, however, whatever your flaws and or weaknesses may be, understand God still chose you to be used for His glory and to come forth with greatness.

Believe in your greatness. What are some of the ways God has made you great through Him?

My late Bishop Dr. David B. Gates II said, "God doesn't respond to your fears, but God responds to your faith."

These words are very well put and true. Mark 5:36 says, "As soon as Jesus heard the word that was spoken, he Saith unto the ruler of the synagogue, be not afraid, only believe." (KJV)

The Word of God is our blueprint to our destiny. Psalm 119:105 says, "Thy word is a lamp unto our feet, and a light unto our path." (KJV) Therefore, when we don't trust what God says and how He leads us, then we are setting ourselves up to miss out on the amazing plan and eternal blessings that God has predestined for them that believe.

> **Hebrews 11:1-13, KJV**– *Now faith is the substance of things hoped for, the evidence of things not seen. For by it the elders obtained a good report. Through faith we understand that the worlds were framed by the word of God, so that things which are seen were not made of things which do appear. By faith Abel offered unto God a more excellent sacrifice than Cain, by which he obtained witness that he was righteous, God testifying of his gifts: and by it he being dead yet speaketh. By faith Enoch was translated that he should not see death; and was not found, because God had translated him: for before his translation he had this testimony, that he pleased God. But without faith it is impossible to please him: for he that cometh to God must believe that he is, and that he is a rewarder of them that diligently seek him. By faith Noah, being warned of God of things not seen as yet, moved with fear, prepared an ark to the saving of his house; by the which he condemned the world, and became heir of the righteousness which is by faith. By faith Abraham, when he was called to go out into a place which he should after receive for an inheritance, obeyed; and he went out, not knowing whither he went. By faith he sojourned in the land of promise, as in a strange country, dwelling in tabernacles with Isaac and Jacob, the heirs with him of the same promise: For*

*he looked for a city which hath foundations, whose builder
and maker is God. Through faith also Sara herself received
strength to conceive seed, and was delivered of a child when
she was past age, because she judged him faithful who had
promised. Therefore sprang there even of one, and him as
good as dead, so many as the stars of the sky in multitude,
and as the sand which is by the sea shore innumerable. These
all died in faith, not having received the promises, but having
seen them afar off, and were persuaded of them, and
embraced them, and confessed that they were strangers and
pilgrims on the earth.*

Notice in Hebrews 11:1-13 that faith is the way to see the manifestation of greatness and the promises of God.

Based on Abel's sacrifice to that of Sarah's conception of a child, this verifies that faith is what God responded to back then, and faith is what God will respond to now. But the decision is up to man to believe, not only in the death burial and resurrection of Jesus Christ (Luke 26:46-47), but to stretch one's faith further and believe in what God says to do.

In Genesis 12:1-10, it shows that when we trust what God's says, it will also open up a door to many blessings.

Genesis 12:1-10, MSG *– Now the Lord had said unto
Abram, Get thee out of thy country, and from thy kindred,
and from thy father's house, unto a land that I will shew
thee: And I will make of thee a great nation, and I will bless
thee, and make thy name great; and thou shalt be a blessing:
And I will bless them that bless thee, and curse him that
curseth thee: and in thee shall all families of the earth be
blessed. So Abram departed, as the Lord had spoken unto
him; and Lot went with him: and Abram was seventy and
five years old when he departed out of Haran. And Abram*

took Sarai his wife, and Lot his brother's son, and all their
substance that they had gathered, and the souls that they had
gotten in Haran; and they went forth to go into the land of
Canaan; and into the land of Canaan they came. And
Abram passed through the land unto the place of Sichem,
unto the plain of Moreh. And the Canaanite was then in
the land. And the Lord appeared unto Abram, and said,
Unto thy seed will I give this land: and there builded he an
altar unto the Lord, who appeared unto him. And he
removed from thence unto a mountain on the east of Bethel,
and pitched his tent, having Bethel on the west, and Hai on
the east: and there he builded an altar unto the Lord, and
called upon the name of the Lord. And Abram journeyed,
going on still toward the south. And there was a famine in
the land: and Abram went down into Egypt to sojourn there;
for the famine was grievous in the land.

Before God blessed Abram, there were three significant matters that took place. One was the instructions that Abram received and his response to God. When the Lord instructed Abram to leave his country, his family and his father's home, to go to a land that God would show him, God didn't give all the details about the land.

Abram could have questioned God, asking the Lord why. Why leave where he resided? Why leave his family? And why leave his country at the age of 75? But in Genesis 12, there is no verse that says Abram questioned God. Instead, in verses 4-5, it says that Abram followed the instructions of God and departed out of his country with his family and went to the land of Canaan.

However, ideally when God gives us an instruction to move, or go in any given direction, perhaps we may question God why. Because His instructions don't make sense to us at the time. As humans, we'd rather understand the logic behind making a move.

For instance, whenever I'm in the passenger seat of a car, and the driver makes a turn one way, as a passenger, sometimes I think to myself, *Why didn't the driver go the other way?* And, similar to my walk with God, when God says He wants me to go in a certain direction, I may wonder, *Why this way, Lord?*

However, whenever I analyze God's direction, I also have to check my level of faith. If I say I believe in what God says, then I realize I should not be questioning God. For when we don't question God, this proves our faith and enables us to receive the promises of God.

In Hebrews 11:1-13, the second significant matter was the promise God Gave Abram, which consisted of three separate promises:

1. The Lord would bless him by making Abram's name great by making him a great nation, and by blessing those that bless him, and by cursing those that curse him, and that through Abram all the families of the earth would be blessed. (Genesis 12:2-3)

2. The Lord would give the land of Canaan unto Abram his seed forever. (Genesis 13:15)

3. God would keep him safe and give Abram a great reward. (Genesis 15:1)

For sure, these promises were a load of greatness for Abram and for those connected to him. But in order to obtain them, Abram had to trust God the entire way.

Like Abram, so shall it be with us. Before we can obtain the promise, we have go the way God leads us and also believe God the entire time. The more we can't comprehend God's Way, I believe the bigger the promise God gives for trusting in what He says.

When we look at Genesis 12, Abram's trust in God not only led him to journey in different places in Canaan, but in his journey, he came across an obstacle—famine (a barrenness) in the land. And this obstacle was the third important matter in Genesis 12:1-10.

The famine in Canaan was an obstacle sent by God, not only to punish the iniquity of the Canaanites who dwelt there, but to exercise the faith of Abram. For God wanted to use the famine as a way to strengthen Abram's belief in Him.

From time to time, God will use obstacles along the way that will help us stay strong in believing in Him. James 1:3 says, "Know that the testing of your faith produces perseverance." (KJV)

Just like we naturally need to routinely exercise for our body to stay fit, we spiritually need our faith to be exercised to stay spiritually fit in believing. For anytime you have submitted to God's way and an obstacle comes along, just encourage yourself by saying, "I'm just exercising my faith."

When Abram entered into this famine, I imagine that he could have turned around and decided to go back to his home. Instead, Abram choose to go through this place of barrenness and trust God. Thereafter, Abram traveled to Egypt where he had another uneasy encounter with a man name Pharaoh.

When Abram arrived in Egypt, the Bible says in Genesis 12:11-12 that he instructed Sarai (Abram's wife) to lie and say she was his sister and not his wife. Abram believed that because of Sarai's beauty, this lie would protect him from being killed and prevent Sarai from being taken away by pharaoh.

Before Pharaoh heard of this lie, due to Sarai's beauty, he took Abram and Sarai into his home and treated them well. He gave them sheep, oxen, asses, and camels. But then the Lord sent a plague upon Pharaoh's house because of Abram's lie. (Genesis 12:15-17)

> **Genesis 12:18, KJV** – *And Pharaoh called Abram, and said, what is this thou hast done unto me? Why didn't thou not tell me she was thy wife?*

And this affliction against Pharaoh forced him to throw both Abram and Sarai out of his home, with all they were given, with no possible desire for Pharaoh to try to take Sarai as his wife. (Genesis 12:19-20)

Although Abram sinned by telling a lie, God covered Abram with a plague with the purpose of saving the promises He gave Abram, because Abram was walking by faith.

As we trust God, we will see that in our journey with Him. There is a method to the Lord's madness. We may not always understand the madness, but as it unfolds, faith will reveal that God is in control and that God will keep His promise.

Paul says it best in Romans 8:28, "And we know that for those who love God, all things work together for good, for those that are called according to his purpose." (ESV)

After Pharaoh commanded that Abram, Sari, and his family go away, the things that Abram had been given at Pharaoh's house, he was able to take with him. And with these things, Abram became very rich, loaded with cattle, silver, gold, and tents, for he left with many possessions. For the promise of God blessing Abram was being fulfilled, and the Lord had more blessings in store.

God told Abram in Genesis 13:14-17, "Open your eyes, look around. Look north, south, east, and west. Everything you see, the whole land spread out before you, I will give to you and your children forever. I'll make your descendants like dust—counting your descendants will be as impossible as counting the dust of the Earth. So—on your feet, get moving! Walk through the country, its length and breadth; I'm giving it all to you." (MSG)

Notice, in Genesis 13:15, God promised He would not only give Abram the land of Canaan, but also give it to Abram's seed. Within Genesis 13:16, God gave another promise that Abram's wife Sari would bear a child.

Genesis 15:2-5, KJV – Abram said, "God, Master, what use are your gifts as long as I'm childless and Eliezer of Damascus is going to inherit everything?" Abram continued, "See, you've given me no children, and now a mere house servant is going to get it all."

Then God's Message came: "Don't worry, he won't be your heir; a son from your body will be your heir." Then he took him outside and said, "Look at the sky. Count the stars. Can you do it? Count your descendants! You're going to have a big family, Abram!"

The promise of Abram's wife having a child at an old age was unbelievable to any human being. Before, Abram believed on this promise, he thought of his age and the land of Canaan, and how much longer he would possibly live to see it. His question to God in Genesis 15:3 shows the humanity of his thinking, that Abram didn't see himself living to do the impossible. Nevertheless, he chose to believe God and God said Abraham was righteous because he believed. (Genesis 15:6)

Because Abram chose to believe God in spite of what seem impossible, God proved through Abram and his wife Sarai that what may seem impossible to man is not impossible to God.

> ***Matthew 19:26, KJV*** *– But Jesus beheld them and said unto them, with men this is impossible; but with God all things are possible.*

In Genesis 16-21, God proved His word to be true and He fulfilled the promise He gave to Abram, showing that with God, nothing is impossible. For Abraham had eight sons, and by this time, his name had already been changed from Abram, because God declared him to be a father of many nations. (Genesis 17:5-6)

Abraham had his first son, Ishmael, birthed from Hagar. (Genesis 16:15-16) And thereafter, when Abraham was ninety-nine years old, Sarah (whose name changed from Sarai), miraculously became pregnant at eighty-nine .

Isaac was the name of the son that Abraham and Sarah had together. (Genesis 21:2-3) And Abraham's six other sons were by Keturah, another wife.

Genesis 25:1-2, KJV – Then again Abraham took a wife, and her name was Keturah.

And she bare him Zimran, and Jokshan, and Medan, and Midian, and Ishbak, and Shuah.

Abraham had a son that Sarah bore, and Abraham had more children than the stars he counted when God made covenant with Him. (Genesis 15:1-18).

There's a song I learned in Sunday School when I was six years old, and the lyrics say, "Father Abraham had many sons, and many sons had Father Abraham, I am one of them, and so are you so let's just praise the Lord." The key words in this song are, "I am one of them, and so are you."

This song connects with the promise that God gave specifying that all the families of the earth through Abraham will be blessed. Therefore, the covenant God made to Abraham includes both you and I.

Romans 4:16-17, 20, NIV – Therefore, the promise comes by faith, so that it may be by grace and may be guaranteed to all Abraham's offspring—not only to those who are of the law but also to those who have the faith of Abraham. He is the father of us all. As it is written: 'I have made you a father of many nations.' He is our father in the sight of God, in whom he believed—the God who gives life to the dead and calls into being things that were not. Yet he did not waver through unbelief regarding the promise of God, but was strengthened in his faith and gave glory to God.

Based on these verses, Abraham set the example of how to receive the promises of God. The example he set for us is to have faith.

By believing in what God says, we can surely obtain the promises that God has given. Whether it be the individual promises God has made to each of us, or the same promise that God gave us through Abraham.

Therefore, on your journey to coming forth with greatness, faith is going to be the key. For faith is a weapon that will overcome every obstacle and defeat any attack that comes against the path to your destiny.

Use faith as a weapon. How are you using faith as a weapon right now? If you aren't, how can you start?

> ***Ephesians 6:10-11,16, NIV*** *– Finally, be strong in the Lord and in his mighty power. 11 Put on the full armor of God, so that you can take your stand against the devil's schemes. 16 In addition to all this, take up the shield of faith, with which you can extinguish all the flaming arrows of the evil one.*

Based on these verses in Ephesians 6:10-11,16, I believe God is giving three main points:

1. Put on the armor of God.
2. Faith will give you power.
3. God's shield of faith will spiritually fight for you.

Shields are used to intercept specific attacks, whether from close-ranged weaponry or projectiles, as well as to provide passive protection closing one or more lines of engagement during combat. (Wikipedia Dictionary)

And just as a shield is used in the natural, the shield of faith is used the same way. The only difference is the shield of faith is used for a different style of combat—spiritual warfare (Ephesians 6:12), where we can't actually see in human-form the devil and his devices but with God's spiritual discernment, He gives us the ability to see in the spirit.

Psalm 119:66 says, "Teach me good judgement and knowledge, for I believe in your commandments." (NKJV) And by testing you may discern what is the will of God, what is that good, acceptable and perfect will of God. (Romans12:2b KJV)

In other words, although as followers of God, we encounter spiritual warfare, we don't have to be blind-sided by the enemy. My pastor Dr. Jacqueline R. Gates once said, "Fight with the wisdom (knowledge and understanding) of God, and be equipped with the necessary tools through the spirit of God to avoid being deceived."

In the same way you shower, dress, and eat before you leave your home in the morning, the same should be with faith. Make the routine of putting on the shield of faith before you go off into your day. It's like the American Express credit card commercial says: "Don't leave home without it." The same applies for your destiny in Christ—don't leave home without your faith.

Remember, everything you need to give birth to your greatness and to fulfill your purpose in God's plan depends upon your submission to God's word and your faith. It's up to God to do the rest.

Now, below is a prayer of faith. When you finish praying, I challenge you from this day forward to let nothing stop you from reaching your destiny in Christ Jesus.

Prayer of Faith

Father, in the name of Jesus, I confess that I am a sinner. I ask that you forgive me for my sins. I believe you died on the cross for my sins, was buried, and rose from the dead. I thank You for my salvation (Romans 10:9).

Father, Your Word says that if I have faith, I will receive whatever I pray for. (Matthew 21:22) So with faith I ask in your name that you would help me in my journey to greatness for Your glory. I ask that You would lead me and guide me, for I choose not to lean to my own understanding (Proverbs 3:5-6), for I trust You, Lord.

You have given me gifts, talents, ministry, and purpose, and my desire is to use what You have given me, according to Your will and way. I believe whatever test, attack, or obstacle that may come in my path, that God, You will lift up a standard and protect me. (Isaiah 59:19)

And I believe through Your strength that I can endure all things through Your power. (Philippians 4:13) God, I thank You for being with me always, even unto the end of the world. (Matthew 28:20) I thank You that the righteous shall live by faith, prevail, and inherit the kingdom of God. (Romans 1:7, Matthew 5:10)

Father, I praise You and I ask all these things in Your Son's name. Amen.

Now, decree and declare, I am a midwife and no matter what; I will not let my seed of greatness die, but live.

About the Author

Antenia Simmons is an Elder in the Gospel that serves in her local church. Her call and gift of preaching and writing several Gospel stage plays has encouraged and inspired many to trust in God's word and to not give up on the plan of God. She has written and produced stage plays such as, "Safe in His Arms," "The Heart of a King," "It Can Be Done," and "Confidence."

CPSIA information can be obtained
at www.ICGtesting.com
Printed in the USA
BVHW041428160621
609642BV00005B/1179